Also by the American Heart Association

AMERICAN HEART ASSOCIATION
LOW-SALT COOKBOOK

AMERICAN HEART ASSOCIATION
LOW-FAT, LOW-CHOLESTEROL COOKBOOK

AMERICAN HEART ASSOCIATION
FAT AND CHOLESTEROL COUNTER

AMERICAN HEART ASSOCIATION
COOKBOOK, Fifth Edition

AMERICAN HEART ASSOCIATION
FAMILY GUIDE TO STROKE
TREATMENT, RECOVERY, AND PREVENTION

American Heart Association

KIDS'
COOKBOOK

A
SPECIAL
MEMBER
BENEFIT
FROM
AAL

TIMES **T** BOOKS

RANDOM HOUSE

American Heart Association

KIDS'
COOKBOOK

Edited by
Mary Winston, Ed.D., R.D.

With a Special Message from
James H. Moller, M.D.

Illustrated by
Joan Holub

Your contribution to the American Heart Association supports research that helps make publications like this possible. For more information, call 1-800-AHA-USA1.

Library of Congress Cataloging-in-Publication Data

American Heart Association kids' cookbook/edited by Mary Winston; with a special message from James Moller. — 1st ed.
     p.   cm.
     Includes index.
     Summary: A cookbook of recipes for snacks, soups, salads, entrees, desserts and other dishes that are healthy and easy to make.
     ISBN 0-8129-1930-0
     1. Cookery — Juvenile literature.   [1. Cookery.]   I. Winston, Mary.   II. American Heart Association.   III. Title: Kid's cookbook.
TX652.5.A453   1992
641.5'123 — dc20   91-50596

Manufactured in the United States of America   9 8 7 6 5 4 3 2
First Edition
                                        Designed by Roberta V. Pressel

ACKNOWLEDGMENTS

Deputy Vice President for Medical and Scientific Affairs
Rodman D. Starke, M.D.

Editor
Mary Winston, Senior Science Consultant, Scientific Affairs

Managing Editor
Jane Ruehl

Recipe Development
Patricia E. Dahl
Gail Greene

Writer
Patricia Cobe

Illustrator
Joan Holub

Education Consultant
Cecil Pretty

Recipe Analysis
Nutrition Coordinating Center, University of Minnesota at Minneapolis

The *American Heart Association Kids' Cookbook* came to be only as a result of the skillful blending of a variety of talents. Chief among them is Dr. James H. Moller, professor of pediatrics at the University of Minnesota and a member of the American Heart Association Board of Directors, whose contributions helped shape this book into a great resource about the role of diet in preventing heart disease. With her keen eye for detail, her ability to simplify the most complex of sentences and merge the most diverse of writing styles, Jane Ruehl is the very valuable managing editor. Because of Cecil Pretty, a master child educator, knowledgeable about and sensitive to the varying levels of children's abilities and skills, the book is custom designed for those eight to twelve years of age. Patricia Cobe's appealing writing style will capture the fancy of these children. Our talented food stylists, Trish Dahl and Gail Greene, created the tasty recipes that we think kids will find hard to resist.

A special thank you to Cheryl Bates for keeping the lines of communications open between all of the project participants and the publisher. Without the careful behind-the-scene contract negotiations skillfully performed by Sam Inman, vice president of corporate relations, and Ann Yanosky, corporate relations specialist, there could be no book. Thanks also to Dr. Rodman D. Starke, deputy vice president for medical and scientific affairs, for his enthusiasm for the project and his wonderful suggestions that helped make it a better book.

Never to be forgotten are Gerre Gilford and Debra Bond, who tirelessly and without complaint typed and retyped the manuscript until it became a perfect whole.

The project was made more enjoyable and easier to accomplish by the never failing support of my son, Rick, and Jane's daughters, Jennifer and Alissa.

There are many others too numerous to mention whose support and suggestions contributed to this book. To them, I am deeply grateful.

Mary Winston, *Editor*

CONTENTS

CALLING ALL COOKS

What room in your house can offer the most excitement and adventure? Any votes for the kitchen? That's our choice! We think it can be a play room, family room, and cooking lab all rolled into one.

Some of you might have already discovered the magic and fun hidden within the nooks and crannies of your kitchen. For others, this room might still be mysterious, uncharted territory, just waiting to be explored. Whatever your experience has been, we think you will enjoy using this book to learn how to cook some terrific meals. A few pots and pans, a well-stocked fridge, and a little know-how can add up to lots of good times and good eating. We'll show you how.

Just reading through the recipes in this cookbook might make you hungry enough to run to the stove and immediately start cooking! But before you begin, we'd like you to take a close look at some important information we've gathered for you. Some of this information is on the next few pages. Even more can be found on pages 97–123. We've given you information on the kitchen tools, cooking techniques, safety tips, and healthy eating hints you'll need to become a smart cook. Read these through by yourself first, then talk them over with the grown-ups in your family. Once you all feel comfortable with these basics, you'll be ready to get going.

The next step is to choose a recipe you'd like to try. We included some of your all-time favorites. You'll find recipes for chicken nuggets, pizza, tortillas, spaghetti, and shakes. We also tried to tempt your taste buds with some new creations, like Spicy Buttons and Bows, Baked Potato Soup, Cinnamon-Raisin Scones, and Hidden Treasure Cake.

As you prepare the recipes in this cookbook, you'll be learning how to make smart food choices that you can stick with for the rest of your life. You'll also be picking up valuable kitchen skills that will come in handy now and later—when you're out on your own. These are two big steps toward becoming a responsible, independent person. Most of all, you'll be having fun making wonderful food to share with your family and friends. They'll be proud you're a "pro"—and you'll be proud of yourself!

GETTING READY TO COOK AND SAFETY CHECKLIST

Are you ready to start cooking? Let's roll up our sleeves and get going.

Before You Start

- Choose a recipe just right for your age and cooking ability. Our symbols will help you. If the skill level of the recipe shows one chef's hat, that means the recipe is easy to prepare. Those recipes with two chef's hats are just a little more challenging, and so on. The most complex recipes—the ones with three chef's hats—are designed for slightly older kids with some cooking experience.
- Read the recipe through carefully. If there's a word or direction you don't understand, check "Cook's Chatter" on pages 114–117. If you're still puzzled, ask a grown-up or older sister or brother to explain it.
- Gather all the ingredients and equipment you'll need for the recipe. Organized cooks have a much easier time preparing a recipe and cleaning up later on.
- Read the "Safety Checklist" below. Go over every item on the list with a grown-up so everyone feels confident.
- While these recipes were designed for kids, some steps require more grown-up help than others. Every time you see this symbol, it means you should ask a grown-up to give you a hand. And never be shy about asking for help *whenever* you may need it.
- Put on an apron to protect your clothes. If you have long hair, tie it back so it doesn't fall into the food or a cooking pot.
- Wash your hands with soap and water and dry them well.

Safety Checklist

The kitchen can be the most fun room in the house, but you do need to be careful

there. Read through this checklist carefully with a grown-up before you begin.

In the Kitchen

- Ask your parents to post a list of emergency numbers near the phone. Be sure they include the numbers for the local fire

department, police department, and poison control center. They should also list the family doctor, a close relative, and a neighbor.
- Have a first aid kit handy in a kitchen cabinet or drawer. Ask a grown-up to help you if you get a nick or burn.
- Keep a fire extinguisher near the stove for dousing small fires.
- Learn the "Stop, Drop, and Roll" rule if your clothes should catch on fire: *Stop* running, *drop* to the ground, and *roll* to extinguish the flames.
- If you get a minor burn, hold it under cold water from the faucet for several minutes. Never put butter or any kind of grease on a burn.

For Food Preparation

- Always handle food with clean hands and clean utensils.

- Be very careful when you're cutting with sharp knives. Always pick up a knife by its handle, never by its blade.
- If a recipe requires chopping or slicing, use a cutting board and have a grown-up stand by to supervise. Place the food to be cut on the board and hold it down on one end. Hold the knife in your other hand and cut down slowly and carefully, pointing the blade away from you.
- When you're finished using a knife, set it aside to wash separately. Don't throw a knife into a sink filled with soapy water. You could reach in later and accidentally cut yourself.
- Make sure your hands are completely dry before plugging in or unplugging an electrical appliance.
- Never put your hands near the beaters of an electric mixer while it's running.
- Never open a food processor until it stops turning.
- Set aside food processor blades to wash separately. These can be as dangerously sharp as knives.
- Keep younger brothers and sisters out of the way of sharp knives and electrical appliances. But it might be fun (with parents' permission) to let them help with simple tasks, such as tearing lettuce for a salad, setting the table, or mixing ingredients in a bowl.

For Cooking
- Keep clean, dry oven mitts next to the stove and oven. Always use them to hold pot handles when stirring, to pick up pots from the stove, and to take things in and out of the oven and microwave.
- When cooking on top of the stove, turn all pot handles toward the center. Never let handles stick over the edge of the stove. Someone might bump into the handles and tilt the pot over or get burned.
- Do not use vegetable oil spray near an open flame or a heat source. Spray a pot or pan far away from the stove. Read the label and follow the instructions very carefully.
- Use a wooden spoon or a metal spoon with a wooden or plastic handle to stir the contents of a pot. An all-metal spoon

can get too hot and burn your fingers.
- When you lift the lid off a pot, be sure to point it away from your face. Otherwise, the hot steam that escapes can burn you.
- Turn off the oven or burners on the stove as soon as you finish cooking.
- Set hot pots and pans on a heatproof board, a trivet, or a wire cooling rack—never directly on the countertop.

For the Microwave
- Make sure you understand how to work your microwave oven. Ask a grown-up to go through the steps with you so you will know how to operate it safely.
- If you cannot reach the microwave door or controls, ask a grown-up to help you. Don't stand on a stool or chair to put food in, take food out, or set the controls of the microwave.
- Do not turn on a microwave oven when it's empty. This can damage the appliance. Try keeping a cup of water in the microwave when it's not being used for cooking. The water can prevent possible damage if the microwave is accidentally turned on.
- Be sure to use only utensils and cookware that are safe for the microwave oven. Metal pans, foil containers, and some other types of dishes can cause sparks and create a fire hazard. Many of the newer microwaveable utensils are now labeled "safe for microwave use." Check with a grown-up to be sure which utensils are safe to use in the microwave.
- Even microwave-safe dishes can get hot from the heat of the food. Always use oven mitts to remove dishes from the microwave or when stirring hot foods in the oven.
- Never stand close in front of the oven door to watch the food cook. Step away from the microwave and listen for the timer to tell you when the food is ready. Food cooked in the microwave continues to cook after it is removed. So let the food stand a few minutes before testing for doneness.
- Open covered or sealed dishes very slowly to avoid burns from the hot steam. Always tilt the dish cover away from your

face and hands.

- If you cover a dish with plastic wrap, don't allow the wrap to touch the food directly as you heat it. It can melt into the food. Always "vent" or turn up a corner of the plastic wrap so steam can escape. When you're finished cooking, never pierce the plastic wrap with a sharp point, such as a fork or knife tip. The escaping steam can burn you.
- Use extreme caution when opening a bag of microwave-popped corn. Hot steam will escape when you open the popcorn. So be sure to point the top of the bag away from you.
- Do not eat microwaved food right after taking it from the oven. Foods cooked in the microwave sometimes have hot spots that can burn your mouth and throat. Let the food stand for a few minutes to cool. Then stir, if possible, to distribute the heat before tasting.

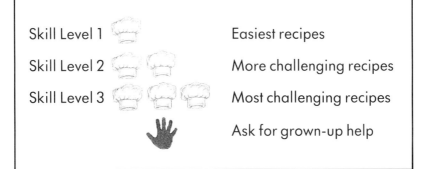

Skill Level 1   Easiest recipes

Skill Level 2   More challenging recipes

Skill Level 3   Most challenging recipes

Ask for grown-up help

RECIPES

SNACKS

Pop Snack
Nutty Pineapple Nibbles
Tortilla Crisps
Mexi Dip Olé

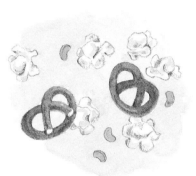

If you think snacking is a bad idea, think again. Munching between meals can be a healthy pastime—providing you choose nutritious, low-fat nibbles.

Next time your tummy feels a little empty, reach for one of the homemade snacks in this chapter instead of grabbing a bag of chips or a handful of store-bought cookies. Such tasty treats as Tortilla Crisps with Mexi Dip Olé and Nutty Pineapple Nibbles pack in lots of nutrients but very little fat. And you can easily make up a batch of these snacks ahead of time to have on hand when hunger strikes. What's more, each of these recipes makes plenty to share with family and friends!

POP SNACK

Serves 2; approximately 1½ cups per serving *Skill Level: 1*

This is so delicious, it will disappear in no time. If you are serving more than two people, make double the recipe. Just toss together twice the amount of each ingredient in a large bowl. If there is any left over, you can scoop small portions of it into resealable plastic bags. Then take a bag to school for a healthy lunch-time treat.

▶ INGREDIENTS

1 package light microwave popcorn
¼ cup dried apples, peaches, or other favorite dried fruit
½ cup small, unsalted pretzels
¼ cup dry-roasted, unsalted peanuts
¼ cup raisins

▶ EQUIPMENT

Oven mitts
Measuring cups
Large bowl
Kitchen scissors
Wooden spoon

▶ INSTRUCTIONS

1 Pop corn in microwave oven as directed on package. Use oven mitts to remove bag from oven. Open very carefully, turning bag opening away from your face.

2 Measure 1½ to 2 cups popcorn into bowl.

3 With kitchen scissors, cut dried apples, peaches, or other favorite dried fruit into ¼-inch pieces.

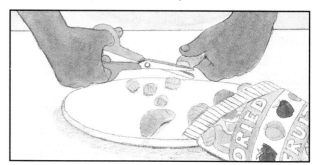

4 Add dried fruit to popcorn.

5 Add pretzels, peanuts, and raisins to popcorn mixture.

6 Using wooden spoon, toss to mix. Serve at once.

▶ COOK'S NOTE

Instead of microwave popcorn, you may substitute 1½ to 2 cups of any unbuttered, unsalted popcorn. You can buy it in a package or make it yourself in an air popper.

NUTTY PINEAPPLE NIBBLES

Serves 10; 3 pieces per serving

Skill Level: 1

*Are you looking for a party snack that will wow your friends? Then make a batch of these.
You can even make them ahead and keep them in the refrigerator till party time.*

▶ INGREDIENTS

6 10-inch celery stalks
¼ cup canned crushed pineapple
½ cup soft "light" cream cheese
2 tablespoons creamy peanut butter
1 tablespoon honey
¼ cup raisins or dried fruit bits
¼ teaspoon hot pepper sauce
  (optional)
3 tablespoons dry-roasted,
  finely crushed nuts

▶ EQUIPMENT

Paper towels
Small, sharp knife
Cutting board
Medium strainer
Measuring cups
Measuring spoons
Medium bowl
Rubber spatula
Table knife
Large plate or serving tray

▶ INSTRUCTIONS

1 Rinse celery stalks and dry with paper towels.

2 Put stalks on cutting board. With small, sharp knife, trim leafy parts off celery stalks.

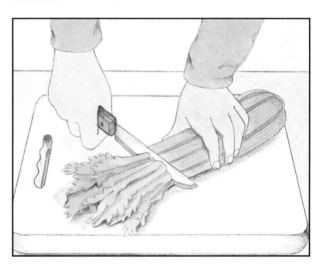

3 Drain pineapple well in strainer.

4 In medium bowl, combine drained pineapple, cream cheese, peanut butter, and honey. Stir with rubber spatula until well mixed. Stir in raisins or fruit bits and hot sauce, if desired.

5 With table knife, fill groove of each celery stalk with cheese mixture.

6 Sprinkle crushed nuts over celery stalks.

7 Place filled celery stalks on large plate or serving tray.

8 Refrigerate for 30 minutes, uncovered.

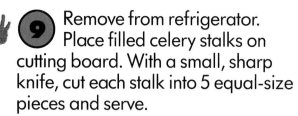

9 Remove from refrigerator. Place filled celery stalks on cutting board. With a small, sharp knife, cut each stalk into 5 equal-size pieces and serve.

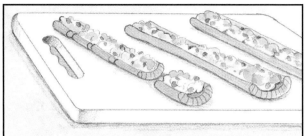

▶ **C O O K ' S   N O T E**

Soft "light" cream cheese is packaged in a tub container. It is sold in the dairy case of your supermarket.

T O R T I L L A   C R I S P S

Serves 6; 8 pieces per serving

Skill Level: **1**

The tortilla chips you buy in a bag are sometimes oily and salty. Our homemade chips are baked instead of fried and only lightly salted. We think you'll agree that they are just as crispy and hard-to-resist as store-bought ones. And they're good for you too!

▶ **I N G R E D I E N T S**

12 6-inch corn tortillas
Vegetable oil spray
½ teaspoon salt

▶ **E Q U I P M E N T**

Cutting board (12 x 18 inches or larger)
Measuring spoons
Chef's knife or pizza cutter
Baking sheet or cookie sheet
Oven mitts
Wire cooling rack
Resealable plastic bag or airtight container

▶ **I N S T R U C T I O N S**

1 Preheat oven to 400° F.

2 Lay 6 tortillas on cutting board. Spray tortillas with vegetable oil spray. Sprinkle ⅛ teaspoon salt lightly over all tortillas.

3 Turn tortillas over; spray and lightly salt the other sides as in step 2.

4 Place tortillas in a stack. With chef's

knife or pizza cutter, cut stack into four pieces, forming triangles or wedges.

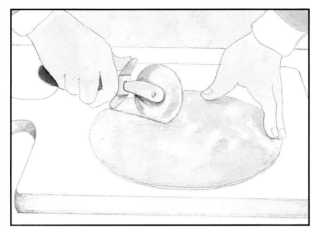

5 Lay tortilla quarters out in one layer on unsprayed baking sheet or cookie sheet.

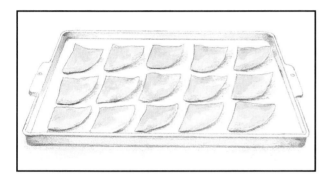

6 Spray, salt, and cut remaining tortillas as in steps 2, 3, and 4. Lay quarters on baking sheet.

7 Place baking sheet in pre-heated oven. Bake chips 8 to 9 minutes, or until they are crisp.

8 With oven mitts, remove baking sheet or cookie sheet from oven to wire cooling rack. Serve chips immediately with Mexi Dip Olé. Or, let chips cool completely and store in sealed plastic bag or airtight container.

► **V A R I A T I O N**

Leave out salt. Lay 6 tortillas on cutting board. Spray with vegetable oil spray; then sprinkle ¾ teaspoon Mexican seasoning over all the tortillas. Then turn them over, spray, and season the other sides with another ¾ teaspoon seasoning. Repeat with the other 6 tortillas.

MEXI DIP OLÉ

Serves 6; approximately ¼ cup per serving   *Skill Level: 2*

One bite of this zesty dip will remind you of all the sunny flavors of Mexico. For a party, set the dip on a pretty heatproof tray or platter surrounded by Tortilla Crisps for dunking. If the grown-ups in your family can't stay away, promise you'll make some for their next get-together!

▶ INGREDIENTS

Vegetable oil spray
1 9-ounce can bean dip (select a dip that does not have lard on the ingredients list)
3 green onions (scallions)
4 ounces sharp, low-fat cheddar cheese (1 cup grated)
2 to 3 small tomatoes
6 tablespoons light sour cream
Sprigs of parsley

▶ EQUIPMENT

9-inch shallow, ovenproof dish
Can opener
Rubber spatula
Cutting board
Chef's knife or kitchen scissors
Measuring cups
Small bowl
Grater and bowl (optional)
Small, sharp knife
Oven mitts
Wire cooling rack
Measuring spoons

▶ INSTRUCTIONS

1 Preheat oven to 400° F.

2 Spray dish with vegetable oil spray.

3 Open can of bean dip. With rubber spatula, spread dip over bottom of dish.

4 Rinse and slice green portions of onions (see page 21). Throw away white part. Measure ¼ cup onion slices into small bowl.

5 Grate cheese if it is not preshredded (see page 21).

6 Add grated cheese to green onions and mix well. Sprinkle mixture evenly over bean dip.

7 Place dish in preheated oven. Bake, uncovered, for 7 to 10 minutes, or until cheese is bubbly.

8 While mixture is baking, rinse tomatoes and pat dry. Place each tomato on cutting board. With a small, sharp knife, cut out core from each tomato. Cut in half and remove seeds and pulp. Dice tomatoes into ¼-inch pieces. Measure ⅔ cup tomatoes and set aside.

 9 With oven mitts, remove dish from oven when cheese is bubbly. Place dish on cooling rack.

10 Sprinkle diced tomatoes over cheese.

11 Top with 6 dollops (small mounds) of sour cream, each measuring 1 tablespoon. Add parsley.

12 Serve immediately with Tortilla Crisps (see pages 18–19).

▶ **C O O K ' S   N O T E**

Italian plum tomatoes, also known as Roma tomatoes, work well in this recipe. These egg-shaped tomatoes are firm and easy to handle.

▶ **M I C R O W A V E**

I N S T R U C T I O N S

Heat onion, cheese, and bean mixture on HIGH (100% power), uncovered, for 3 minutes. Continue with the regular recipe at step 8.

▶ **C O O K ' S   N O T E**

How do you slice a green onion? Easy—just follow these directions:
● Rinse green onions and place on cutting board.
● With chef's knife or kitchen scissors, cut off stringy roots and tips of green shoots.
● With one hand, hold white part of onion on cutting board. (You may cut one, two, or three onions at a time.)
● With chef's knife or kitchen scissors, slice green portions of onions into thin slices.
● Stop cutting when you reach the white part.
● If the recipe uses green portions only, throw away the white part.
● If the recipe uses green and white portions, continue cutting until you are near the end.
● Ask a grown-up to assist you the first few times.

▶ **C O O K ' S   N O T E**

Low-fat cheddar cheese comes in wedges or sticks in your supermarket's dairy case. You may also buy already shredded low-fat cheese in plastic packages or bags. You can pour the shredded cheese right from the package into the measuring cup. To grate your own cheese, follow these directions:
● Place the grater in a bowl.
● Hold the grater firmly in one hand and place a large piece of cheese in other hand.
● Rub the cheese against the small holes of the grater. (The cheese will come out in shreds.)
● Be careful not to rub your knuckles against the grater.
● Ask a grown-up to help you the first few times.

SOUPS AND SALADS

Grandpa's Favorite Soup
Garden Patch Soup
Baked Potato Soup
Sunshine Slaw
Shimmering Fruit Salad

The recipes in this chapter are wonderful "menu makers." A soup and salad together can serve as a satisfying supper or filling lunch. Or you can start a family dinner with Baked Potato Soup or Garden Patch Soup, then serve Sunshine Slaw as a side dish. The combination of fresh ingredients in each recipe offers a healthy addition to any meal.

If you're a beginning cook, it's best to follow these soup and salad recipes exactly. But as your cooking skills improve, you might want to experiment a little. Vary the vegetables in Grandpa's Favorite Soup, choosing your own favorites. Or try grapefruit in the Shimmering Fruit Salad instead of orange. Both the soup pot and salad bowl allow lots of room for creativity.

GRANDPA'S FAVORITE SOUP

Serves 10; 1 cup per serving

Skill Level: 2

Here's a soup that can be the star of the dinner table, especially on a cold winter's night. And you can be the star of the house when you cook it yourself.

▶ INGREDIENTS

1 large onion
2 tablespoons corn oil
1½ pounds extra-lean stew beef,
    cut into ¾-inch cubes,
    trimmed of all visible fat
1 14½-ounce can beef broth
1 medium potato
2 medium carrots
2 cups tomato juice
1½ cups frozen kernel corn
1 cup frozen cut green beans
1 14½-ounce can diced tomatoes
    in juice
1 tablespoon dried basil leaves
1 teaspoon dried thyme leaves
½ to 1 teaspoon coarsely ground
    black pepper
½ teaspoon garlic powder
½ teaspoon salt (optional)

▶ EQUIPMENT

Cutting board
Small, sharp knife
Chef's knife
Large saucepan or Dutch oven
    (4- to 6-quart size), with cover
Measuring spoons
Wooden spoon
Can opener
Vegetable peeler
Measuring cups
Ladle

▶ INSTRUCTIONS

1 Peel and chop onion (see page 25).

2 Pour oil into saucepan or Dutch oven. Place pan on burner. Turn heat to medium. Heat oil for 1 minute.

3 Add chopped onion. Cook 5 to 7 minutes, or until onion turns almost clear. Stir often with wooden spoon.

4 Raise heat on burner to high. Add meat cubes to onion. Cook about 5 minutes, turning and stirring with spoon, until beef is evenly browned and all meat juices have evaporated.

⑤ Stir in beef broth. Cover pan and lower heat to medium. Cook for 55 to 60 minutes, or until beef cubes are tender when pierced with a fork. (Be sure to lift the cover of the pan away from your face when you check the beef cubes.)

⑥ While meat is cooking, peel potato and carrots with vegetable peeler.

⑦ Place potato on cutting board. Using chef's knife, dice (cut) potato into ½-inch pieces.

⑧ Place carrots on cutting board. Using chef's knife, cut carrots into thin slices.

⑨ When meat is ready, add potatoes, carrots, and all other ingredients. Cover pan and cook over medium heat about 20 minutes, or until potato cubes are tender.

⑩ Use ladle to pour soup into bowls. Serve hot.

▶ **COOK'S NOTE**

You may freeze half this recipe for another meal. Let soup cool in pot until it's no longer hot to the touch. Then use a ladle to transfer leftover soup into a 2-quart freezer container with a cover. Cover and place in freezer.

▶ **COOK'S NOTE**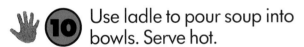

It's especially important to use extra-lean beef in this recipe. The butcher can trim off the excess fat for you, or you can do it in your own kitchen. Cut the beef into cubes. Place the beef cubes on the cutting board.

With a small, sharp knife, cut off any fat you see on the outside of the meat. (You might want to have a grown-up help you with this step.) Once the meat is in the soup pot, be sure to wash the knife and cutting board thoroughly with hot, soapy water before using it for other ingredients.

▶ **COOK'S NOTE**

Chopping onions doesn't have to bring tears to your eyes. Here's how to do it:
- With a small, sharp knife, cut off both ends of the onion.
- Peel away the outer, papery layers of the onion with your hands while holding the onion under cold running water. Place the onion on the cutting board. Throw away the peel.
- Cut the onion in half from top to bottom.
- Place the onion halves cut-sides down on the cutting board.
- Holding one onion half on the board with one hand and a chef's knife in the other, cut the onion half crosswise into several slices from top to bottom.

- Cut across the slices lengthwise about 5 or 6 times to form small, square pieces about ¼ inch each.

- Repeat with the other half of the onion.
- Ask a grown-up to assist you the first few times you chop.

GARDEN PATCH SOUP

Serves 6; 1 cup per serving

Skill Level: **2**

A bunch of fresh broccoli looks a lot like a flowering tree. The dark green flowers on top of the stalks are sometimes called "florets." When a recipe calls for "broccoli florets," here's what you do. Place the whole bunch of broccoli on a cutting board. With a sharp knife, cut off flower along with the thin piece of stem attached to it. Then measure and cut the florets as directed in the recipe. Save the "trunk" and "branches" of the broccoli tree for another use.

▶ INGREDIENTS

1 large onion
2 tablespoons margarine
8 ounces fresh mushrooms
¼ teaspoon ground white pepper
½ teaspoon salt (optional)
2 medium carrots
3 14½-ounce cans chicken broth
½ cup (2 ounces) uncooked
   miniature shell pasta
1 cup broccoli florets
1 tablespoon chopped fresh parsley

▶ EQUIPMENT

Cutting board
Small, sharp knife
Chef's knife
Large saucepan or Dutch oven
   (4- to 6-quart size), with cover
Wooden spoon
Small cloth or paper towels
Measuring spoons
Vegetable peeler
Measuring cups
Ladle

▶ INSTRUCTIONS

1 Peel and chop onion (see page 25).

2 Put margarine into saucepan or Dutch oven. Place on burner. Turn heat to medium-high and cook until margarine melts.

3 Add chopped onion. Cover and cook for 5 to 7 minutes, or until onion turns almost clear, stirring occasionally with wooden spoon.

4 Wipe mushrooms with a clean, damp cloth or paper towels. Place mushrooms on cutting board. With a small, sharp knife, cut mushrooms into thin slices.

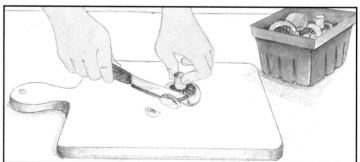

5 Add mushrooms to pan. Add pepper and salt, if you like.

6 Lower heat to medium. Cover and cook 10 minutes.

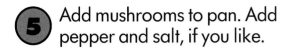 **7** With vegetable peeler, peel carrots and place on cutting board. With chef's knife, cut carrots into thin slices.

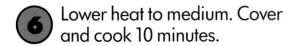 **8** Uncover pan. Add carrots, chicken broth, and pasta. Cook, uncovered, over medium heat 10 minutes longer.

9 Place broccoli florets on cutting board. With chef's knife, cut into ½-inch pieces.

10 Stir broccoli and parsley into soup. Cook, uncovered, over medium heat for 5 minutes more.

11 Use a ladle to pour soup into bowls. Serve hot.

BAKED POTATO SOUP

Serves 3; 1¼ cups per serving

Skill Level: 2

Do you like baked potatoes topped with sour cream, chives, and bacon? Then you'll love this soup! It has the same great taste, but it's lower in fat and cholesterol. The light sour cream, low-fat cheese, and imitation bacon bits used in this recipe make the difference.

▶ INGREDIENTS

2 medium (8- to 9-ounce) baking potatoes
1 ounce low-fat colby or cheddar cheese (¼ cup grated)
1 14½-ounce can chicken broth
2 tablespoons light sour cream
⅛ teaspoon ground black pepper
1 green onion (scallion) (optional)
1 tablespoon imitation bacon bits

▶ EQUIPMENT

Vegetable brush
Paper towels
Fork
Aluminum foil
Grater and bowl (optional)
Measuring cups
Oven mitts
Cutting board
Small, sharp knife
Can opener
Electric blender
Heavy saucepan
Wooden spoon
Measuring spoons
Chef's knife or kitchen scissors
   (optional)
Ladle

▶ INSTRUCTIONS

1 Preheat oven to 350° F.

2 Scrub potatoes with vegetable brush and pat dry with paper towels.

🖐 **3** Pierce each potato five or six times with a fork and wrap in aluminum foil.

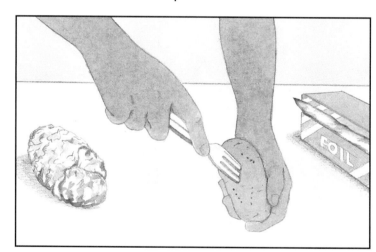

🖐 **4** Place wrapped potatoes in oven. Bake for 1 hour.

🖐 **5** Meanwhile, grate cheese if it is not preshredded (see page 21). Cover cheese and set aside.

6 Using oven mitts, remove potatoes from oven. Let rest in foil 15 to 20 minutes.

7 Carefully remove foil from potatoes. Be careful of steam! Allow potatoes to cool slightly. Peel potatoes with hands.

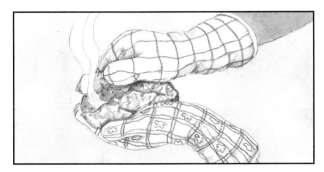

8 Place one potato on cutting board. With small, sharp knife, cut potato into 4 pieces.

9 Place the cut potato and the chicken broth in blender. Cover and blend on high speed until smooth.

10 Pour potato mixture into the saucepan.

11 Place second potato on cutting board. With small, sharp knife, dice potato into cubes. Stir diced potato, sour cream, and ground pepper into saucepan.

12 Place saucepan on burner. Turn heat to low. Cook soup until hot and steaming. Do *not* boil.

13 Meanwhile, rinse and cut green portion of onion (see page 21). Throw away white part. Place green onion slices in a small dish to use as topping for soup.

14 Place cheese and bacon bits in separate small dishes to use as toppings for soup.

15 To serve, ladle soup into bowls.

16 Sprinkle with choice of toppings.

► MICROWAVE INSTRUCTIONS

- Scrub potatoes and pierce each potato one time with fork.
- Wrap potatoes in paper towels. Microwave on HIGH (100% power) 8 minutes.
- Using oven mitts, turn potatoes over. Cook 2 to 3 minutes longer. Use oven mitts to check for doneness. Potatoes should feel soft but slightly firm.
- Remove potatoes from microwave and wrap in aluminum foil. Let rest 15 to 20 minutes. Go back to step 7 and continue with the rest of the recipe.

► DID YOU KNOW?

Imitation bacon bits are made from soybeans, and they are seasoned to taste like real bacon. But since they're not a meat product, they contain just a trace of fat and no cholesterol. They are available in jars and at supermarket salad bars.

S U N S H I N E   S L A W

Serves 5; ½ cup per serving   *Skill Level:* 1

This crunchy, vitamin-packed mix of carrots and cabbage will delight you and your family. You can shred the vegetables yourself by rubbing them against the large holes of a metal grater or shredder. (If you have a food processor, you can get the same results in less time by using the metal shredding blade. Be sure a grown-up is nearby to supervise. The metal blade is very sharp.) You can also save time by buying already shredded cabbage and carrots in the produce section of some supermarkets. Look for them in plastic bags or at the salad bar.

► INGREDIENTS

2 cups shredded carrots
(approximately 4–6 medium)
2 cups shredded red cabbage
(approximately 1 small head)
1 orange, unpeeled
1 6-ounce container low-fat orange
or lemon yogurt
⅛ teaspoon salt
6 tablespoons unsalted, dry-roasted peanuts
½ cup drained mandarin orange sections,
canned in light syrup

► EQUIPMENT

Measuring cups
Medium bowl
Grater
Small bowl
Measuring spoons
Wooden spoon
Can opener
Medium strainer
Rubber spatula
Plastic wrap (optional)

▶ I N S T R U C T I O N S

1 Place shredded carrots and cabbage in medium bowl. With clean hands, mix thoroughly. When finished, wash and dry hands.

2 Rinse orange. Using grater, rub orange against smallest holes to form very fine pieces of orange peel. Measure ¼ teaspoon grated rind into small bowl.

3 Add yogurt and salt to orange rind. Stir well with wooden spoon.

4 Add yogurt mixture to carrot-cabbage mixture. Stir until well combined.

5 Add peanuts to yogurt-vegetable mixture. Stir until all ingredients are completely mixed.

6 Drain mandarin orange sections in strainer. Measure ½ cup and add to bowl. Gently mix in orange sections with rubber spatula. (Using the rubber spatula helps to keep the orange sections from breaking.)

7 Serve immediately. Or cover with plastic wrap and refrigerate until serving time.

▶ C O O K ' S   N O T E

After grating the orange peel, separate the orange into sections. Wrap with plastic wrap or place in a small plastic bag. Refrigerate to enjoy later as a snack or dessert.

SHIMMERING FRUIT SALAD

Serves 5; 1 cup per serving

Skill Level: **3**

*This is a colorful and pretty combination of fruit to enjoy as a salad, snack, or dessert.
Everyone will be impressed with the fancy way you cut up the fresh fruit.*

▶ INGREDIENTS

1 21-ounce can peach pie filling
1 medium orange
½ large Red Delicious apple
1 cup cantaloupe chunks
1 cup seedless green grapes, rinsed
½ cup seedless red grapes, rinsed
1 medium banana

▶ EQUIPMENT

Can opener
Large bowl
Rubber spatula
Small, sharp knife
Serrated knife
Cutting board
Measuring cups
Fork
Plastic wrap
Soup spoon

▶ INSTRUCTIONS

1 Empty can of peach pie filling into bowl, scraping inside of can with rubber spatula to remove all of glaze.

2 With small, sharp knife, cut a small circle from top of orange, *leaving one edge attached*. With a sawing motion, cut around orange, forming a spiral of peel. Turn the orange in your hand as you cut. Cut off any remaining spots of white pith left on the orange.

3 With serrated knife, cut orange in half from top to bottom. Place flat side on cutting board and slice orange thinly. Remove seeds. Add orange slices to bowl with peach pie filling.

4 Cut the half-apple lengthwise into ½-inch thick slices. Remove seeds and core. Cut each slice into triangles. (The red skin should be at the bottom of each triangle.)

5 Add apple slices, cantaloupe chunks, and green and red grapes to bowl with pie filling.

6 Peel banana. Draw tines of fork from tip to tip along the edge of the peeled banana to "score" the surface. Slice "scored" banana into bowl with pie filling.

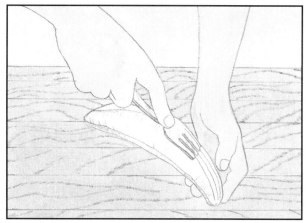

7 With rubber spatula, gently mix fruits. Cover with plastic wrap and refrigerate several hours before serving.

8 To serve, spoon fruit salad onto small dishes or plates.

▶ **VARIATION**

Add ⅓ cup unsalted, dry-roasted pecan halves to finished salad.

ENTRÉES

Shake-It-Up Chicken Nuggets
Polka Dot Chicken Pasta Salad
Mexican Sombreros
Tasty Turkey Chili
Microwave Lemon Fish
Tamale Beef Squares
Pasgetti Spaghetti
Broiled Italian Meatballs
Top Hat Pizza
Spicy Buttons and Bows

"Entrée" is the French word for "main course." In a typical American meal, the main course is usually chicken, meat, or fish. Some of the recipes in this chapter do include these foods, but others focus on pasta or pizza for the main course. You'll see some of your favorite dinner foods here, such as spaghetti with meatballs, chili, and chicken nuggets. But you'll learn how to make them in healthier, lower-fat ways.

For example, Shake-It-Up Chicken Nuggets begin with skinless chicken breasts and are baked in the oven, not fried in oil. In Tasty Turkey Chili, ground turkey stands in for beef. Tamale Beef Squares prove there's a place for red meat in a heart-healthful diet, provided the meat is lean. And Top Hat Pizza and Spicy Buttons and Bows show that meatless entrées can make a hearty main course. Every one of these dishes fits into the new, low-fat, low- cholesterol guidelines we recommend...but all are very high in taste and enjoyment too.

SHAKE-IT-UP CHICKEN NUGGETS

Serves 4; 4 nuggets per serving

Skill Level: 3

Chicken nuggets are usually deep-fried in hot oil to give them a crispy coating. But all that oil makes the nuggets greasy. In our recipe, the chicken is tossed in a bag with seasoned stuffing mix and grated Parmesan cheese. It is then baked in the oven. These "oven-fried" nuggets are crisp and golden. But, they don't have that extra fat you get from deep-frying.

▶ INGREDIENTS

1¾ cups herb-seasoned crumb stuffing mix
¼ cup grated Parmesan cheese
3 tablespoons margarine
¼ cup low-fat buttermilk
¼ teaspoon ground black pepper
2 boneless, skinless chicken breasts
    (approximately 1 pound)

▶ EQUIPMENT

Measuring cups
Resealable plastic bag (1 gallon size)
Rolling pin
Small saucepan or small microwave-
    safe bowl and wax paper
Measuring spoons
Medium shallow bowl
Mixing spoon
Paper towels
Cutting board
Small, sharp knife
Baking sheet
Oven mitts
Tongs

▶ INSTRUCTIONS

1 Preheat oven to 450° F.

2 Measure stuffing mix into resealable plastic bag. Seal bag and place on flat surface. Crush crumbs by rolling and pressing rolling pin over bag.

3 Open bag and add Parmesan cheese. Reseal bag and shake to mix thoroughly.

4 Melt margarine (see page 37).

5 Place melted margarine, buttermilk, and pepper in medium shallow bowl. Stir well with spoon. Set aside.

6 Rinse chicken breasts and pat dry with paper towels.

7 Place chicken breasts on cutting board. Cut chicken with small, sharp knife into 16 chunks of the same size. (Each chicken breast should give you 8 chunks or pieces.)

8 Dip each chicken chunk into buttermilk mixture, covering all sides. Let extra buttermilk mixture drip off. Place 3 dipped chunks at a time into bag of crumbs. Seal bag tightly and shake until chicken pieces are evenly coated with crumbs.

9 Place coated nuggets on an ungreased baking sheet. Repeat with remaining chicken chunks.

10 Place baking sheet in oven. Bake nuggets 4 minutes.

11 With oven mitts, remove pan from oven. Using tongs, turn over each nugget.

12 Return to oven and bake 4 to 5 minutes, or until medium golden brown.

13 With oven mitts, remove pan from oven. Using tongs, remove nuggets to platter or plates. Serve nuggets immediately. Place a small bowl of your favorite dipping sauce nearby, if you like.

▶ COOK'S NOTE

You may buy boneless chicken breasts with skin on and remove the skin, or buy skinless, boneless chicken breasts.

▶ DID YOU KNOW?

The buttermilk you buy in the supermarket is not full of butter, even though it sounds like it might be. Actually, buttermilk is low in fat and cholesterol. It's made from skim milk. However, buttermilk is thicker than skim milk, and it has a slightly tangy taste. It helps the coating stick to these chicken nuggets and gives them a real country flavor.

▶ COOK'S NOTE

You can use the stovetop or the microwave to melt margarine. If you choose a stick margarine, it can easily be measured by looking at the tablespoon markings on the wrapper and cutting off the amount you need. Each stick equals 8 tablespoons. To melt the margarine, follow these easy steps:

▶ STOVETOP

- Place margarine in small saucepan.
- Place saucepan on burner.
- Turn heat to low.
- Heat until margarine melts, stirring occasionally.

▶ MICROWAVE

- Place margarine in small microwave-safe bowl.
- Cover with wax paper.
- Microwave on HIGH (100% power) 30 to 45 seconds for 1 tablespoon, or 45 to 60 seconds for ¼ cup.

POLKA DOT CHICKEN PASTA SALAD

Serves 6; 1 cup per serving

Skill Level: **3**

Remember the food groups in our "Guidelines for a Low-Fat, Low-Cholesterol Diet" on page 104–105? Here is one recipe that combines foods from several of these food groups. There's pasta from the starchy foods group, chicken from the meat group, yogurt from the milk and cheese group, and plenty of vegetables and fruits from that group. All in all, this makes for lots of variety and delicious, nutritious eating.

▶ INGREDIENTS

6 ounces uncooked no-egg pasta, any shape
   (rigatoni, rotini, shells, elbows macaroni, etc.)
   (½ of a 12-ounce package or 1 cup)
1 cup cooked chicken or turkey, skin and fat
   removed, cut into ½-inch chunks
1 Red Delicious apple, unpeeled and rinsed
1 tablespoon lemon juice
1 celery stalk
3 green onions (scallions)
1 medium carrot
¾ cup drained pineapple tidbits,
   canned in fruit juice
½ cup raisins
¾ cup low-fat lemon yogurt
¼ cup reduced-calorie mayonnaise
¾ teaspoon grated lemon rind
¼ teaspoon salt
⅛ teaspoon ground white pepper
Lettuce (optional)

▶ EQUIPMENT

Large pot
Measuring cups
Colander
Oven mitts
Large bowl
Wooden spoon
Cutting board
Small, sharp knife
Small bowl
Paper towels
Measuring spoons
Chef's knife
Kitchen scissors (optional)
Vegetable peeler
Grater
Can opener
Strainer
Medium bowl
Wire whisk
Rubber spatula
Plastic wrap

▶ I N S T R U C T I O N S

1 Fill large pot with water as directed on pasta package. Place pot on burner. Turn heat to high and bring water to a boil.

2 Add pasta to boiling water. Cook according to package directions, leaving out salt and butter or margarine.

3 Place colander in sink. With oven mitts, remove pot to sink. Pour pasta into colander. (Be careful that boiling water does not splash on you.) Rinse pasta with cold water to stop pasta from cooking any more. Drain pasta again in colander.

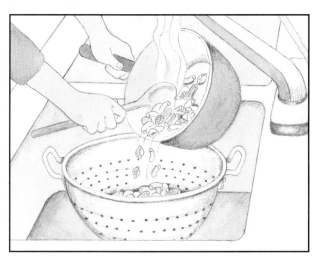

4 Pour drained pasta into large bowl. Add chicken and, with a wooden spoon, toss to combine. Set aside.

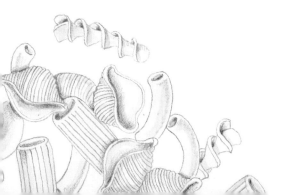

5 Place apple on cutting board. With small, sharp knife, cut apple into quarters. Make a lengthwise cut along inside of each quarter to remove core and seeds.

6 Cut apple into ¾-inch chunks. Place chunks in small bowl. Add lemon juice and toss apples to coat evenly with juice.

7 Rinse celery and dry with paper towels. Place celery on cutting board and cut into thin slices with chef's knife. You should have about ½ cup.

8 Rinse and cut green portions of onions (see page 21). Throw away white part. Measure ¼ cup onion slices.

9 Add apple, celery, and green onions to pasta; toss to combine.

10 With vegetable peeler, peel carrot. Cut ¼ inch off each end of carrot with small, sharp knife. Coarsely grate carrot by rubbing it against large holes of grater. Add carrot to pasta mixture.

11 Place pineapple in strainer and drain well. Measure ¾ cup. Add drained pineapple to pasta.

12 Add raisins to pasta; toss to combine.

13 In medium bowl, combine yogurt, mayonnaise, lemon rind, salt, and pepper for dressing. Mix with wire whisk until evenly blended.

14 Add dressing to pasta mixture. With rubber spatula, mix until well combined. Cover bowl with plastic wrap. Refrigerate salad for several hours before serving. Serve on a bed of lettuce, if desired.

▶ **COOK'S NOTE**

Tossing the apple pieces with lemon juice helps keep them from turning brown.

The grated lemon rind used in this recipe is a ready-made spice available in your supermarket.

MEXICAN SOMBREROS

Serves 6; 1 sombrero per serving

Skill Level: **3**

Microwave Oven Required

In Mexico many people wear large straw hats called "sombreros" to protect them against the strong sun. These zesty, hat-shaped treats won't work well as head gear, but they sure taste terrific! The secret is a lively blend of Mexican-style seasonings and lean turkey, baked in the oven and topped with chunky salsa and melted cheese. Yum!

▶ **INGREDIENTS**

½ green bell pepper
½ small onion
1 tablespoon water
1 slice whole-wheat bread, crust removed
1 tablespoon skim milk
1 pound fresh ground turkey
   (ground without skin)
2 teaspoons dried parsley flakes

2 tablespoons mild taco seasoning mix
1 teaspoon chili powder
Vegetable oil spray
6 6-inch soft corn tortillas
   (select tortillas that do not have
   lard on the ingredients list)
1 ounce sharp, low-fat cheddar cheese
   (¼ cup grated)
6 teaspoons mild chunky salsa

▶ E Q U I P M E N T

Cutting board
Small, sharp knife
Chef's knife
Small microwave-safe bowl
Measuring spoons
Wax paper
Medium bowl
Wooden spoon
Jumbo muffin pan cups or
    6 6-ounce (3½-by-2-inches)
    ovenproof glass custard cups
Kitchen scissors
Aluminum foil
Oven mitts
Grater and bowl (optional)
Measuring cup
Soup spoon

▶ I N S T R U C T I O N S

1 Rinse green pepper and place on cutting board. Cut pepper in half. Remove seeds and white pith from inside the pepper. With small, sharp knife, chop green pepper.

2 Peel and chop onion (see page 25).

3 In small microwave-safe bowl, mix green pepper, onions, and water. Cover with wax paper.

4 Microwave on HIGH (100% power) for 4 minutes. Let cool in microwave oven.

5 Preheat oven to 350° F.

6 Into medium bowl, crumble bread into small pieces. Add milk and let stand for 3 to 4 minutes. Stir with wooden spoon until blended.

7 With clean hands, crumble turkey into bread mixture.

8 Add parsley, taco seasoning, chili powder, and cooked pepper and onion. Mix well with hands or wooden spoon.

41

9 Spray muffin pan cups or custard cups with vegetable oil spray.

10 With kitchen scissors, cut 4 slashes in each tortilla from the edge toward the center.

Fit tortillas into muffin pan cups or custard cups, overlapping cuts like a flower.

11 Divide the turkey mixture evenly over the tortillas.

12 Cover with foil and place muffin pan or cups in oven. Bake for 30 minutes.

13 Using oven mitts, remove from oven and let rest, covered, for 5 minutes. Carefully remove foil from pan or cups.

14 Meanwhile, grate cheese if it is not preshredded (see page 21). Set aside.

15 To serve, use a soup spoon to remove sombreros from muffin pan or cups and place on plates. Spoon 1 teaspoon salsa on top of each sombrero. Top each with a rounded teaspoon of grated cheese.

▶ **C O O K ' S   N O T E**

Ask your butcher to help you select turkey ground without skin. Serve this recipe with a nice green vegetable or a salad for a complete meal.

▶ **D I D   Y O U   K N O W ?**

Chili powder is a blend of several spices. It usually contains cumin, oregano, and dried chili peppers. It comes in both "mild" and "hot" flavors. What you use depends on how spicy you like your chili!

TASTY TURKEY CHILI

Serves 8; 1 cup per serving

Skill Level: 2

Beans have a lot going for them! They're high in protein and fiber, but they are very low in fat. They also contain many vitamins and minerals. That's how they help stretch 1¼ pounds of turkey into a main dish that feeds 8 hungry people. Besides, what would a genuine bowl of chili be without beans? We used pintos and black beans here. But you can substitute kidney beans, chickpeas, or your own favorites. Why not cook up a pot of chili for your family one Sunday night soon?

▶ INGREDIENTS

1 large onion
2 tablespoons corn oil
1¼ pounds fresh ground turkey
    (ground without skin)
½ teaspoon garlic powder or 2 large
    cloves garlic, peeled and minced
2 teaspoons chili powder
½ teaspoon ground black pepper
½ teaspoon ground cumin
1 15-ounce can pinto beans
1 15-ounce can black beans
1 14½-ounce can diced tomatoes
    in juice, undrained
1 6-ounce can tomato paste
1 14½-ounce can chicken broth
1 cup frozen corn kernels
4 to 5 green onions (scallions)

▶ EQUIPMENT

Small, sharp knife
Cutting board
Chef's knife
Dutch oven or large saucepan with cover

Measuring spoons
Wooden spoon
Can opener
Strainer
Measuring cups
Kitchen scissors (optional)
Ladle

▶ INSTRUCTIONS

1 Peel and chop onion (see page 25).

2 Pour oil into Dutch oven or large saucepan. Place pot on burner. Turn heat to medium. Heat oil for 1 minute.

3 Add onions to hot oil. Cook over medium heat, stirring occasionally with wooden spoon, for 5 minutes, or until onion is almost clear.

4 Add ground turkey to pot. Stir with a wooden spoon, breaking up large pieces. Brown turkey for 5 minutes, stirring often.

5 Stir in garlic powder or garlic, chili powder, black pepper, and cumin until well combined.

6 Open cans of pinto and black beans; pour both into large strainer. Place strainer under cold running water. Rinse beans thoroughly and drain.

7 With wooden spoon, stir beans, tomatoes and their juice, tomato paste, chicken broth, and corn into pot. Heat 5 to 7 minutes, or until thoroughly hot, stirring often.

8 Rinse and slice green portions of green onions (see page 21). Throw away white part. You should have about 1/2 cup.

9 Stir green onions into pot. Remove from heat. Ladle hot chili into bowls.

▶ **C O O K ' S   N O T E**

Ask your butcher to help you select turkey ground without skin.

MICROWAVE LEMON FISH

Serves 4; 1 fillet per serving

Skill Level: **2**

Microwave Oven Required

Fish in a flash! Here's a dish that looks fresher and tastes better than frozen fish sticks, yet cooks just as fast. When you buy the crackers for the crumb topping, make sure to choose those made with whole-wheat flour and no saturated fat. Read the ingredient list to be sure. Remember that saturated fat can hide under the names "coconut oil," "palm or palm kernel oil," "lard," "hydrogenated shortening," or "butter."

▶ INGREDIENTS

4 4-ounce orange roughy, cod, haddock, flounder, or other mild fish fillets
¼ teaspoon salt
8 large whole-wheat crackers
2 tablespoons margarine
1½ teaspoons fresh lemon juice
1 tablespoon freshly chopped parsley

▶ EQUIPMENT

Paper towels
Measuring spoons
Microwave-safe baking dish with cover
Electric blender or food processor, or resealable plastic bag and rolling pin
Small saucepan or small microwave-safe bowl and wax paper
Medium bowl
Spoon
Oven mitts
Fork

▶ INSTRUCTIONS

1 Rinse fillets. Pat dry with paper towels.

2 Sprinkle fillets lightly with salt on both sides.

3 Place fillets in one layer in microwave-safe baking dish.

4 Place crackers in blender or food processor. Cover and blend or process until crackers become fine crumbs. Or place crackers in resealable bag. Seal tightly and crush crackers by rolling over them several times with a rolling pin.

5 Melt margarine (see page 37) and place in a medium bowl.

6 Add cracker crumbs, lemon juice, and parsley. Stir to combine well.

7 Sprinkle crumb mixture on top of fish fillets. Cover dish.

8 Microwave on HIGH (100% power) for 6 to 7 minutes. Fish is done when it flakes in the center of fillet when pierced with a fork.

9 Using oven mitts, remove dish from microwave. Uncover dish away from your face. Serve immediately.

TAMALE BEEF SQUARES

Serves 6; 2 squares per serving

Skill Level: **2**

A typical Mexican tamale has a ground meat filling and a cornmeal batter coating. It is then wrapped in a real corn husk. Our version combines the same authentic flavors, but it is much simpler to make. You just spread the cornmeal batter in a baking pan and top it with the meat "filling" and grated cheese. One bite, and friends and family will be shouting, "Olé!"

▶ INGREDIENTS

1 large onion
1 tablespoon margarine
¼ cup water
1 pound ground round
1 tablespoon chili powder
¼ cup drained diced mild green
   chilies (from 1 4-ounce can)
½ teaspoon garlic powder
½ teaspoon salt (optional)
1 14½-ounce can diced tomatoes
   in juice, drained
⅔ cup frozen corn kernels
1 8-ounce package cornbread mix
   (select a mix that does not have
   lard on the ingredients list)
⅓ cup skim milk
1 egg
1 tablespoon corn oil
Vegetable oil spray
4 ounces sharp, low-fat cheddar
   cheese (1 cup grated)

▶ EQUIPMENT

Cutting board
Small, sharp knife
Chef's knife
Medium non-stick skillet
Measuring cups
Wooden spoon
Measuring spoons
Can opener
Strainer
Medium bowl
13-by-9-inch baking pan
Rubber spatula
Oven mitts
Grater and bowl (optional)
Wire cooling rack
Pancake turner or spatula

▶ I N S T R U C T I O N S

(1) Peel and chop onion (see page 25).

(2) Place medium non-stick skillet on burner. Turn heat to medium. Add onion, margarine, and water to skillet. Cook, stirring occasionally with wooden spoon, for 5 to 7 minutes, or until onion turns almost clear.

(3) With clean hands, crumble ground round into skillet. Add chili powder, drained chilies, garlic powder, and salt, if desired.

(4) Cook, uncovered, 8 to 10 minutes over medium heat, stirring often, until meat is browned. As the meat cooks, stir with the wooden spoon to break it up into small pieces.

(5) Stir tomatoes and corn into skillet; remove from heat.

(6) In medium bowl, combine cornbread mix, milk, egg, and corn oil. Stir with a clean wooden spoon just until ingredients are evenly blended.

(7) Preheat oven to 400° F.

(8) Coat baking pan with vegetable oil spray. With rubber spatula, evenly spread cornbread mixture over bottom of pan.

9 With wooden spoon, evenly distribute meat mixture over cornbread layer.

10 Grate cheese if it is not pre-shredded (see page 21). Sprinkle cheddar cheese evenly over meat layer.

11 Place baking pan in hot oven. Bake for 30 to 35 minutes, or until cheese is melted and slightly bubbly.

12 Using oven mitts, remove pan from oven. Place on wire cooling rack or heatproof surface. Let cool a few minutes.

13 With chef's knife, cut into 12 squares. To serve, remove squares from pan with pancake turner. Place 2 squares on each plate.

▶ **C O O K ' S   N O T E**

Ground round is the leanest type of ground beef. Sometimes it is labeled "lean" or "extra lean" on the package. It's best to choose the leanest beef you can find.

PASGETTI SPAGHETTI

Serves 10; 1 cup spaghetti and ½ cup sauce per serving   *Skill Level:* **2**

From the days when you were pronouncing it "pasgetti," you've probably loved this dish. Now that you're calling it "spaghetti" or maybe even "pasta," it's time to learn how to prepare this classic. The sauce has a true Italian taste but doesn't require long simmering or special ingredients.

▶ INGREDIENTS

1 large onion
2 tablespoons olive oil
2 tablespoons water
1 14½-ounce can stewed tomatoes
1 cup water
1 6-ounce can tomato paste
2 teaspoons dried basil leaves
1 teaspoon dried oregano leaves
¾ teaspoon garlic powder
½ teaspoon ground black pepper
1 16-ounce package spaghetti

▶ EQUIPMENT

Cutting board
Small, sharp knife
Chef's knife
Large non-stick skillet
Measuring spoons
Wooden spoon
Can opener
Measuring cups
Large pot
Colander
Oven mitts
Ladle

▶ INSTRUCTIONS

1 Peel and chop onion (see page 25).

2 Pour oil into large non-stick skillet. Add onion and 2 tablespoons water. Place skillet on burner. Turn heat to medium. Stir with a wooden spoon and cook 5 to 7 minutes, or until water boils off (evaporates) and you can hear onion "sizzle" in the oil.

3 Add remaining ingredients, except spaghetti. Lower heat to medium-low. Cook sauce, uncovered, over medium-low heat for 20 minutes, stirring occasionally with wooden spoon.

4 While sauce is cooking, prepare spaghetti in a large pot according to package instructions, leaving out salt and butter or margarine.

5 Place colander in sink. With oven mitts, carry pot of spaghetti from stove to sink. Carefully drain spaghetti in colander. Place about a cup of spaghetti on each plate.

6 Using a ladle, top each serving with ½ cup sauce. Serve hot.

▶ COOK'S NOTE

Freeze 1-cup portions of leftover sauce in microwave-safe containers. To serve, microwave covered portion on DEFROST (30% power) for 3 minutes. Stir. Cover again and microwave on HIGH (100% power) for 3 minutes, or until thoroughly heated.

▶ COOK'S NOTE

Serve with Broiled Italian Meatballs (see pages 52–53).

BROILED ITALIAN MEATBALLS

Serves 5; 3 meatballs per serving

Skill Level: **2**

Do you have younger brothers or sisters who follow you around the kitchen, begging to help you cook? Rolling meatballs is a fun and easy job you can give them. Make sure they start with clean hands. It would also be a good idea for you to stay nearby to lend a hand if needed. Most meatballs are fried in oil before they go into spaghetti sauce. For this recipe, the meatballs are broiled instead—that means less fat and less mess!

▶ INGREDIENTS

1 large onion
1 pound ground round
⅓ cup plain dry bread crumbs
⅓ cup grated Parmesan cheese
⅓ cup evaporated skim milk
1 egg
1½ teaspoons dried Italian herb seasoning
1 teaspoon garlic powder
½ teaspoon salt
½ teaspoon ground black pepper
Vegetable oil spray

▶ EQUIPMENT

Cutting board
Small, sharp knife
Chef's knife
Medium bowl
Measuring cups
Measuring spoons
13-by-9-inch broiler pan or baking pan
Oven mitts
Tongs

▶ INSTRUCTIONS

1 Peel and chop onion (see page 25).

2 In medium bowl, combine chopped onion, ground round, bread crumbs, Parmesan cheese, milk, egg, Italian herb seasoning, garlic powder, salt, and pepper.

3 With clean, dry hands, thoroughly mix together all the ingredients.

4 Rinse your hands with water, but do not dry them. With wet hands, form mixture into 15 meatballs by rolling the meat mixture between the palms of your hands. Each meatball should be about 1¾ inches in diameter. When you're finished rolling the meatballs, wash and dry your hands.

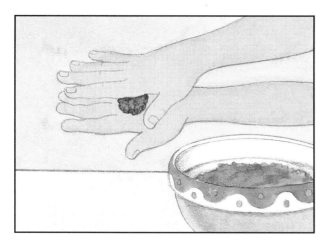

5 Place oven rack 7 inches from broiler. If using broiler pan, remove it from the broiler. Preheat broiler.

6 Spray broiler pan or baking pan with vegetable oil spray. (Make sure you are far away from the broiler while spraying).

7 Arrange meatballs in sprayed pan in 3 rows, 5 meatballs per row.

8 Place pan on oven rack. Broil meatballs 5 minutes.

9 Using oven mitts, remove pan from broiler. With tongs, turn meatballs over.

10 Return pan to broiler. Broil 5 minutes longer. Using oven mitts, remove pan from broiler.

▶ **COOK'S NOTE**

You can serve these meatballs plain, or spoon them into a large non-stick skillet with one half the recipe for Basic Tomato Sauce (see pages 50–51). Place the skillet over medium heat and warm 2 minutes, or until hot.

TOP HAT PIZZA

Serves 1

Skill Level: 2

If you always thought pizza wasn't a nutritious food, think again. This one has a delicious combination of vitamin-packed peppers, low-fat cheese, and whole-wheat bread. It's great for a quick snack, lunch, or supper.

▶ INGREDIENTS

1 7- to 7½-inch round piece whole-wheat pita or pocket bread
3 tablespoons prepared pizza sauce
¼ green or red bell pepper
¼ small onion
⅛ teaspoon dried Italian herb seasoning
½ ounce part-skim mozzarella cheese (2 tablespoons grated)
½ teaspoon grated Parmesan cheese

▶ EQUIPMENT

Cutting board
Small, sharp knife
Chef's knife
Grater and bowl (optional)
Kitchen scissors
Cookie sheet or baking sheet
Oven mitts
Wire cooling rack
Measuring spoons
Small spatula or spoon
Pizza cutter (optional)

▶ INSTRUCTIONS

1 Peel and chop onion (see page 25). Measure out 2 teaspoons and set aside. (Save the rest to use in another recipe.)

2 Rinse bell pepper and place on cutting board. Remove seeds and white pith from inside the pepper. With small, sharp knife, chop bell pepper. Measure out 1 tablespoon and set aside. (Save the rest to use in another recipe.)

3 Grate cheese if it is not pre-shredded (see page 21).

4 Preheat oven to 400° F.

5 Using kitchen scissors, cut out a circle from top layer of the pita bread, leaving 1 inch of top all around to form an edge or border. Save cut-out circle.

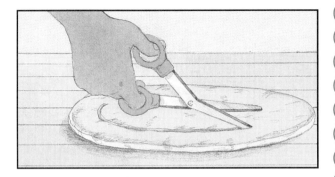

6 Place bottom of pita on cookie sheet or baking sheet. Using oven mitts, put on middle rack in hot oven. Bake 5 minutes.

7 With oven mitts, carefully remove from oven and place pan on wire cooling rack. Cool slightly.

8 Place cooled pita on cutting board. Using small spatula or spoon, spread pizza sauce evenly on top and also under the edge of the pita bread. Sprinkle bell pepper, onion, Italian seasoning, and mozzarella cheese evenly on top of sauce. Top with reserved circle of pita bread to form a "hat."

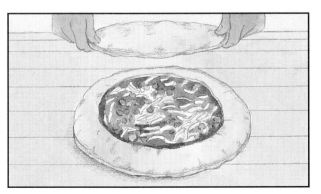

9 Return completed pizza to cookie sheet or baking sheet. Bake in hot oven for 8 to 9 minutes.

10 Carefully remove pan from oven to cooling rack.

11 Sprinkle with Parmesan cheese and let stand a few minutes.

12 Place pizza on cutting board. Cut in half with kitchen scissors, small knife, or pizza cutter. Serve hot.

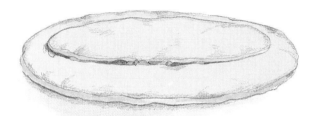

▶ **D I D   Y O U   K N O W ?**

Pita bread came to America from the Middle East. It is used in Turkey, Iran, Syria, Israel, and many other Middle Eastern countries. The bread is often split open to form a "pocket." Meat or vegetables are then stuffed into the pocket to make a sandwich.

SPICY BUTTONS AND BOWS

Serves 6; divided equally

Skill Level: **3**

Microwave Oven Required

Some scholars think pasta originally came from China and was brought back to Italy by the Italian explorer Marco Polo. These days, though, most people consider Italy the birthplace of this popular food. The Italians like to cook pasta until it is "al dente," which translates as "to the tooth." This means it should be tender but still slightly firm, never mushy or soft.

▶ INGREDIENTS

8 cups water
1 teaspoon corn oil
¼ teaspoon salt (optional)
1 cup wagon wheel pasta shapes
¾ cup bow tie pasta shapes
4 ounces mild Mexican processed
   cheese (½ cup cubes)
2 ounces processed cheese spread
   (¼ cup cubes)
1½ tablespoons margarine
1½ tablespoons all-purpose flour
1 cup skim milk, at room temperature
1½ tablespoons chopped fresh parsley
   (optional)

▶ EQUIPMENT

Measuring cups
Large heavy saucepan or Dutch oven
Measuring spoons
Wooden spoon
Colander
Oven mitts

Large bowl
Cutting board
Small, sharp knife
4-cup microwave-safe glass measuring
   cup with handle
Wax paper
Wire whisk

▶ INSTRUCTIONS

1 Measure water into large saucepan or Dutch oven. Place on burner. Turn heat to high. Bring water to a boil.

2 Add oil and salt, if you like, to boiling water. Slowly add pasta. Cook pasta 12 to 14 minutes, or until it is tender, stirring occasionally with wooden spoon.

3 Place colander in sink. With oven mitts, carry pot of pasta from stove to sink. Drain pasta carefully in colander. Rinse with cold water to stop pasta from cooking any more. Drain well. Tranfer pasta to large bowl.

4 While pasta is cooking, place Mexican processed cheese and processed cheese spread on cutting board. Using a small, sharp knife, cut cheese into small cubes. (You should have about ½ cup Mexican cheese cubes and ¼ cup processed cheese spread cubes.) Set aside.

5 Place margarine in microwave-safe glass measuring cup. Cover with wax paper. Microwave on HIGH (100% power) for 30 to 45 seconds, or until melted.

6 Using oven mitts, remove cup carefully from oven.

7 With wire whisk, stir flour into melted margarine. Slowly add milk, stirring well with whisk.

8 Return cup to microwave. Cook on HIGH (100% power) 3 to 4 minutes, stirring after each minute with whisk.

9 Remove cup from microwave and add cubed cheese. Stir until melted.

10 Add cheese mixture to pasta and toss to mix well.

11 If you like, sprinkle parsley on hot pasta before serving.

▶ **COOK'S NOTE**

Water is boiling when lots of bubbles rise to the surface and break. You could also prepare this recipe with about 4 cups left-over cooked pasta.

▶ **DID YOU KNOW?**

Pasta is the general term given to all types of spaghetti, macaroni, and noodles. There are over 600 different shapes of pasta!

VEGETABLES

Nutty Broccoli Flowers
Festive Peas
Confetti-Stuffed Tomato Boats
Oriental Stir-Fry
Speckled Rice

Before you say "yuck" and flip to the next chapter, take a look at these exciting vegetable recipes. Even lifelong vegetable-haters won't be able to resist Confetti-Stuffed Tomato Boats and Festive Peas. No doubt your parents and teachers have told you that vegetables are full of vitamins and other good stuff. But you've probably never realized how great these "nutrition power-houses" could taste! Now's your chance to go beyond plain peas, carrots, and broccoli. Start your explorations right away by turning to the recipes on the next few pages.

NUTTY BROCCOLI FLOWERS

Serves 6; divided equally

Skill Level: 2

As a vegetable, broccoli can't be beaten. It's loaded with vitamin A, vitamin C, and calcium for healthy skin, hair, and bones. It also has good amounts of fiber and iron, and it contains no fat or cholesterol. All this for only about 45 calories a stalk! The almonds and bright red peppers in this recipe add color and crunch.

▶ INGREDIENTS

1 large bunch fresh broccoli
 (approximately 1½ pounds)
1 medium onion
1 large red bell pepper
2 tablespoons margarine
¼ cup water
½ cup sliced almonds
¼ tespoon salt
½ cup water

▶ EQUIPMENT

Cutting board
Small, sharp knife
Colander
Chef's knife
Medium non-stick skillet with cover
Wooden spoon
Measuring cups
Measuring spoons

▶ INSTRUCTIONS

1 Place broccoli on cutting board. With small, sharp knife, trim off ends of broccoli stems to make 3-inch "spears" with florets. Save stem ends of broccoli for another use.

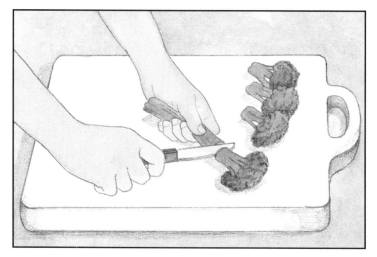

2 Place broccoli spears with florets in colander. Place colander under cold running water. Rinse broccoli, drain well and set aside.

3 Peel and chop onion (see page 25).

4 Rinse red pepper and place on cutting board. Cut pepper in half. Remove seeds and white pith from inside the pepper. Cut into ½-inch pieces with chef's knife. Set aside.

5 Place margarine in medium non-stick skillet. Place skillet on burner. Turn heat to medium. Heat until margarine melts.

6 With wooden spoon, stir chopped onion and ¼ cup water into melted margarine. Cook over medium heat, uncovered, for 3 to 4 minutes, or until water boils off (evaporates).

7 Stir in diced red pepper and almonds. Raise heat on burner to medium-high. Cook mixture, stirring constantly, for 1 minute.

8 Place reserved broccoli spears in one layer on top of onion mixture. Sprinkly broccoli with salt. Add ½ cup water to skillet.

9 Cover skillet. Lower heat to medium. Cook over medium heat for 5 to 7 minutes, or until tip of sharp knife inserted into broccoli spear comes out easily. Serve immediately.

▶ **COOK'S NOTE**

You may purchase trimmed broccoli florets in the produce or salad-bar section of your supermarket. If the broccoli is already trimmed, you will need only ¾ pound.

FESTIVE PEAS

Serves 5; divided equally

Skill Level: **3**

Microwave Oven Required

This recipe has a lively combination of peas, bacon bits, pimiento, green onions, and parsley. These ingredients make this dish colorful and festive. It's great for a family dinner or when company is coming.

▶ INGREDIENTS

2 cups frozen peas
3 tablespoons water
2 green onions (scallions)
2 tablespoons water
2 tablespoons imitation bacon bits
2 teaspoons margarine
1 2-ounce jar chopped pimiento
⅛ teaspoon ground black pepper
⅛ teaspoon ground nutmeg
1½ tablespoons chopped fresh parsley
    (optional)

▶ EQUIPMENT

Measuring cups
Measuring spoons
4-cup microwave-safe glass
    measuring cup with handle
Wax paper
Wooden spoon
Oven mitts
Cutting board
Chef's knife (optional)
Kitchen scissors
Small microwave-safe bowl

Large bowl
Mixing spoon
Strainer

▶ INSTRUCTIONS

1 Place peas and 3 tablespoons water in the microwave-safe glass measuring cup. Cover with wax paper.

2 Microwave on HIGH (100% power) for 2 minutes.

3 Stir peas with wooden spoon.

4 Microwave on HIGH (100% power) another 1½ to 2 minutes, or until cooked through.

5 Using oven mitts, remove peas from microwave to heatproof surface. Stir and set aside.

6 Rinse and slice green portions of onions (see page 21). Set aside. Throw away white part.

7 In small microwave-safe bowl, mix green onions, 2 tablespoons water, bacon bits, and margarine. Cover with wax paper.

8 Microwave on HIGH (100% power) for 1 minute. Let stand in microwave for 3 to 4 minutes to cool.

9 Remove bowl from microwave.

10 Place onion mixture and peas in large bowl. With spoon, toss contents of bowl to mix.

11 Drain pimiento in strainer.

12 Stir drained pimiento, ground pepper, and nutmeg into bowl of peas. Add chopped parsley, if you like. Cover bowl with wax paper.

13 Place in microwave. Cook on HIGH (100% power) for 1 to 2 minutes, or until heated through.

14 Using oven mitts, remove from microwave to heatproof surface. Serve immediately.

▶ **C O O K ' S   N O T E**

The easiest way to cut parsley into tiny pieces is with a pair of kitchen scissors.

CONFETTI-STUFFED TOMATO BOATS

Serves 6; 2 "boats" per serving

Skill level: 2

This fancy vegetable dish will certainly perk up any meal. Notice how it's not necessary to cook the frozen vegetables first. Just run hot water over them to defrost them, and they'll finish cooking as the tomatoes bake. If you're planning to prepare this recipe as a side dish, make sure the rest of your menu is simple. Broiled chicken or fish and plain rice would go well with it.

▶ INGREDIENTS

4 ounces (½ cup) Neufchâtel cheese or light cream cheese
6 fresh, ripe Italian plum tomatoes
Vegetable oil spray
12 dashes ground black pepper (approximately ⅛ teaspoon)
2 tablespoons skim milk
2 ounces sharp, low-fat cheddar cheese (½ cup grated)
4 green onions (scallions)
⅛ teaspoon salt
⅛ teaspoon hot pepper sauce (optional)
1¼ cups frozen mixed vegetables
6 teaspoons grated Parmesan cheese

▶ EQUIPMENT

Medium bowl
Plastic wrap
Cutting board
Small, sharp knife or small, serrated knife
Teaspoon
Medium baking dish
Measuring spoons
Rubber spatula
Grater and bowl (optional)
Measuring cups
Chef's knife or kitchen scissors
Strainer
Oven mitts
Wire cooling rack

▶ INSTRUCTIONS

1 Place Neufchâtel cheese or light cream cheese in medium bowl. Cover with plastic wrap and set aside to let the cheese soften.

2 Place tomatoes on cutting board. With small, sharp knife or small, serrated knife, cut tomatoes in half lengthwise. Use a teaspoon to scoop out seeds and pulp from tomatoes. Throw seeds and pulp away.

3 Spray medium baking dish with vegetable oil spray. Place scooped-out tomatoes in dish, scooped side up. Lightly sprinkle pepper inside each little tomato "boat."

4 Remove plastic wrap from bowl with Neufchâtel cheese. Add milk to softened cheese. With rubber spatula, blend milk into cheese until mixture is well combined and smooth.

5 Grate cheddar cheese if it is not pre-shredded (see page 21). Stir grated cheese into Neufchâtel cheese mixture until well mixed.

6 Rinse and slice green portions of onions (see page 21). Throw away white part.

7 Stir onions and salt into cheese mixture. Stir in hot pepper sauce, if you like. Set mixture aside.

8 Preheat oven to 400° F.

9 Place frozen mixed vegetables in strainer. Run hot water over vegetables until they are thoroughly defrosted, about 1 minute. Drain well.

10 Add vegetables to cheese mixture and blend with rubber spatula.

11 Spoon cheese mixture into the 12 tomato "boats," dividing it evenly. Sprinkle ½ teaspoon Parmesan cheese over each tomato half.

12 Place pan of tomatoes in preheated oven. Bake, uncovered, 25 to 30 minutes, or until tops are golden brown and mixture is bubbly.

13 Using oven mitts, remove pan from oven to wire cooling rack. Let cool for 5 minutes before serving.

▶ **DID YOU KNOW?**

Italian plum tomatoes are sometimes called Roma tomatoes. They have a large amount of pulp and a small number of seeds and juice. This makes them firm and easy to handle.

▶ **COOK'S NOTE**

Neufchâtel cheese is sold in packages in the dairy case. It is lower in fat than cream cheese, but it has a similar taste and works just as well in recipes.

▶ **COOK'S NOTE**

A "dash" of pepper means just a tiny bit—a sprinkle of a few grains.

ORIENTAL STIR-FRY

Serves 4; ½ cup per serving   *Skill Level:* **3**

In stir-frying, food is cooked very quickly over high heat. The ingredients are usually cut into small pieces of the same size so they cook evenly. The most important thing to remember is to constantly stir the pieces of food around as they cook to prevent them from sticking. Stir-frying is typically done in a Chinese-style wok—a round metal pan with sloping sides. If you don't have a wok, a large skillet will work just fine.

▶ INGREDIENTS

1½ cups frozen broccoli florets
   or cut broccoli
1⅓ cups frozen whole baby
   carrots
2 tablespoons honey
1 tablespoon fresh lemon juice
⅛ teaspoon ground allspice
⅛ to ¼ teaspoon ground ginger
Black pepper (optional)
2 teaspoons margarine
1 teaspoon sesame oil
1 green onion (scallion)
   (optional)

▶ EQUIPMENT

Measuring cups
Medium strainer
Paper towels
Cutting board
Small, sharp knife
Chef's knife or
   kitchen scissors
Measuring spoons
Two small bowls
Wok
Oven mitts
Wooden spoon

▶ INSTRUCTIONS

1 Place frozen broccoli and carrots in strainer. Run hot water over vegetables until they are thoroughly defrosted, about 1 minute. Drain well in strainer, then place on paper towels to drain thoroughly. Pat dry with paper towels, if necessary.

2 Place carrots on cutting board. With small, sharp knife, cut carrots into thin diagonal slices.

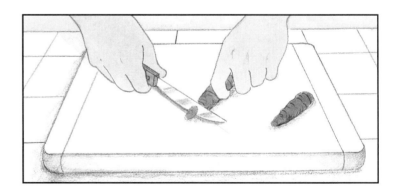

3 Rinse and slice green portions of onion (see page 21). Throw away white part. Measure ½ to 1 teaspoon into a small bowl.

4 Place honey, lemon juice, allspice, ginger, and pepper in another small bowl. Set aside.

5 Place margarine and sesame oil in wok. Place wok on burner. Turn heat to medium-high. Heat margarine and oil until melted and very hot (about 375° F.). Be careful—this is very hot!

6 Carefully add broccoli, carrots, and green onion to wok. Hold handle of wok with pot holder in one hand. Place a wooden spoon in your other hand. Cook vegetables 2 minutes, stirring constantly.

7 Add honey and lemon juice mixture. Cook 2 to 3 minutes longer, stirring constantly. Vegetables should be cooked through but still slightly crisp when done.

8 Serve immediately.

▶ **COOK'S NOTE**

You can buy large bags of frozen broccoli and carrots and measure out the amount you need. Return the remaining vegetables to the freezer before they thaw. Be sure the vegetables are very well drained before cooking so they don't splatter oil when placed in the hot wok.

▶ **DID YOU KNOW?**

Cooking fuel has always been scarce in China. It's no surprise, then, that smart Chinese cooks invented the super-fast method of stir-frying to conserve their precious fuel.

SPECKLED RICE

Serves 6; divided equally

Skill Level: 2

Like pasta, bread, and other grain products, rice is one of those starchy foods that are full of valuable vitamins and minerals. People used to think that starchy foods were fattening. But they aren't. In fact, unless you pile on butter or rich, creamy sauces, they're very low in fat. That's why we should all try to include more starches in our diets. Speckled Rice is a great place to start!

▶ INGREDIENTS

2½ tablespoons margarine
1 cup uncooked long-grain rice
2⅔ cups chicken broth
½ teaspoon ground black pepper
½ teaspoon salt (optional)
6 green onions (scallions)
1 5-ounce package frozen
    chopped spinach (individual
    serving size) or ½ 10-ounce
    package frozen chopped
    spinach, defrosted according
    to package directions

▶ EQUIPMENT

Dutch oven or large saucepan,
    with cover
Measuring cups
Wooden spoon
Can opener
Measuring spoons
Cutting board
Chef's knife or kitchen scissors

▶ INSTRUCTIONS

1 Place margarine in Dutch oven or large saucepan. Place pot on burner. Turn heat to medium. Heat margarine until it melts, about 1 to 2 minutes.

2 Raise heat to medium-high. Add rice. Stir rice constantly with a wooden spoon for 3 minutes.

3 Remove pot from heat. Place on cool burner or heatproof surface. Stir in chicken broth. (Be careful here—steam rises quickly when broth is added to hot rice.)

4 Add pepper and salt, if you like. Cover pot and place over low heat. Cook for 20 minutes, or until rice absorbs all the broth.

5 Meanwhile, rinse and slice green and white portions of onions (see page 21).

6 Remove cover from pot. Stir defrosted spinach and sliced green onions into rice. Serve hot.

► **COOK'S NOTE**

Buy regular long-grain rice for this recipe—not instant, precooked, or parboiled rice.

BREADS

Cheesy Cornbread
Cinnamon-Raisin Scones
Slumber Party French Toast

Eating more grain products and other starchy foods is a smart way to cut back on fat and cholesterol. You'll find this a pleasure to do when the choices are as tempting as these breads. Like pasta, rice, and potatoes, breads are a good source of valuable carbohydrates.

Preparing homemade breads is not as difficult or time-consuming as you may think. The Cinnamon-Raisin Scones and Cheesy Cornbread in this chapter are both known as "quick breads." That means they use baking powder or baking soda to make them rise, and they can be prepared in a flash. Yet they will still fill your house with wonderful baking smells. Don't be surprised if these breads are gobbled up as soon as they come out of the oven!

CHEESY CORNBREAD

Serves 8; 1 wedge per serving

Baked goods such as cornbread, muffins, and banana bread are known as "quick" breads. When making quick breads, remember to lightly stir the dry and wet ingredients together just until they're blended. The dry ingredients should be moistened, and the batter should be slightly lumpy. Mixing the ingredients too much can produce a quick bread that's too dry and tough.

▶ INGREDIENTS

3 ounces low-fat, mild or sharp
  cheddar cheese (2/3 cup
  grated)
2 green onions (scallions)
1 tablespoon margarine
1 8½-ounce box cornbread mix
  (select a mix that does not have
  lard on the ingredient
  list)
⅓ cup skim milk
1 egg
½ cup frozen kernel corn
2 to 3 drops hot pepper sauce
Vegetable oil spray

▶ EQUIPMENT

Grater and bowl (optional)
Cutting board
Chef's knife or kitchen scissors
Measuring spoons
Small saucepan or small
  microwave-safe bowl
  and wax paper

Medium bowl
Oven mitts
Measuring cups
Wooden spoon
Rubber spatula
9-inch glass pie plate
Wire cooling rack
Sharp, serrated knife

▶ INSTRUCTIONS

1 Preheat oven to 400° F.

2 Grate cheese if it is not pre-shredded (see page 21). Set aside.

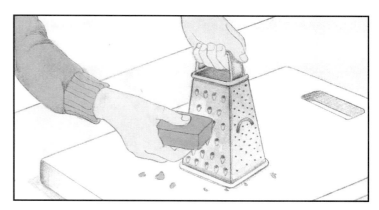

3 Rinse and slice green portions of onions (see page 21). Throw away white part. Measure out 2 tablespoons onion slices and set aside.

4 Melt margarine (see page 37) and place in a medium bowl.

5 Add cornbread mix, milk, and egg. Stir ingredients with a wooden spoon until just evenly blended. Batter should be slightly lumpy. Don't stir too much!

6 Add reserved cheese, green onions, corn, and hot pepper sauce. Mix with spoon until just blended.

7 Spray pie plate with vegetable oil spray until evenly coated.

8 With rubber spatula, spread cornbread mixture evenly in prepared pie plate.

9 Place pie plate in preheated oven. Bake 18 to 20 minutes, or until light golden brown in color.

10 With oven mitts, remove pie plate from oven to wire cooling rack. Let cool for 5 to 10 minutes.

11 Hold pie plate with oven mitts. With sharp, serrated knife, cut cornbread into 8 wedges. Serve warm.

CINNAMON-RAISIN SCONES

Serves 8; 1 scone per serving

Skill Level: 2

This recipe asks you to knead the dough before baking. Kneading is done by placing the dough on a floured board or counter, then pushing and pulling it back and forth several times with your hands. This kneading action helps blend the ingredients thoroughly to produce a smooth dough and tender, mouth-watering scones. They make an irresistible snack or breakfast treat.

▶ INGREDIENTS

1¾ cups all-purpose flour
3 tablespoons sugar
1 tablespoon baking powder
1 teaspoon ground cinnamon
½ teaspoon salt
¼ cup (½ stick) margarine
1 orange, unpeeled
½ cup low-fat buttermilk
1 egg
2 teaspoons vanilla extract
⅓ cup raisins
3 tablespoons all-purpose flour
1 teaspoon sugar
Jam (optional)
Margarine (optional)

▶ EQUIPMENT

Medium mixing bowl
Measuring cups
Measuring spoons
Wooden spoon
Small, sharp knife
Small saucepan or small micro-
    wave-safe bowl and wax paper
Medium bowl
Grater
Baking sheet
Pizza cutter
Oven mitts
Wire cooling rack

▶ INSTRUCTIONS

1 In medium mixing bowl, measure 1¾ cups flour, 3 tablespoons sugar, baking powder, cinnamon, and salt. Mix with wooden spoon for 15 seconds.

2 Melt margarine (see page 37) and place in a medium bowl.

3 Rinse orange. Using grater, rub orange against smallest holes to form very fine pieces of orange peel. Measure ½ teaspoon grated peel into bowl with margarine.

4 Add buttermilk, egg, vanilla extract, and raisins. Stir with wooden spoon for 15 seconds, or until ingredients are blended.

5 Add buttermilk mixture to flour mixture. Stir with wooden spoon 30 to 45 seconds, or until mixture gathers together into a ball.

6 Preheat oven to 425° F.

7 Sprinkle 3 tablespoons flour on a clean surface. Take dough ball from bowl and place on floured surface. Lightly dust your hands with flour.

8 To knead the dough, use the heel of your hand to push the dough away from you slightly. Then, with your hands, pull the dough back toward you, folding it over as you pull it. Repeat this pushing-pulling motion 8 times. (It should take 1½ to 2 minutes.)

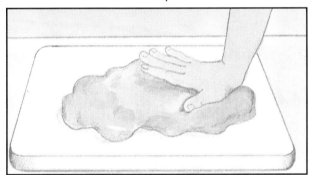

9 Place the kneaded dough on ungreased baking sheet. With your hands, pat the dough out into an 8-inch circle. (You may need to dust your hands lightly again with flour so they don't stick to the dough.) Sprinkle 1 teaspoon sugar on top of dough circle.

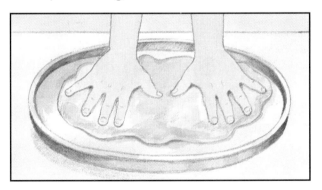

10 Wash and dry hands. With pizza cutter, cut dough circle into 8 wedges. (First cut dough into quarters, then cut each quarter in half.) Slightly separate the dough wedges from each other so they are not touching.

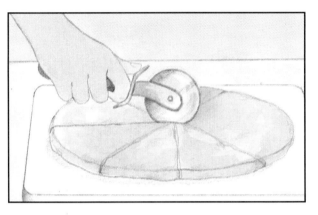

11 Place baking sheet in pre-heated oven. Bake scones for 15 minutes, or until light golden brown.

12 With oven mitts, remove baking sheet from oven to wire cooling rack.

13 Serve scones hot with jam and margarine, if desired.

▶ **DID YOU KNOW?**

Scones are a type of sweet biscuit that originated in England. In British homes, scones are often served along with afternoon tea.

▶ **COOK'S NOTE**

Remember to save the orange sections to eat later.

SLUMBER PARTY FRENCH TOAST

Serves 6; 1 slice per serving

Skill Level: 2

This French toast is a bit different from the usual kind. The bread is first dipped into a sweetened cinnamon-flavored batter, then set in the refrigerator overnight to absorb the delicious flavors. The next morning, it's baked rather than fried. What a way to start the day with sleepover friends or your own family!

▶ INGREDIENTS

¼ cup (½ stick) margarine
½ cup firmly packed dark brown sugar
¾ teaspoon ground cinnamon
Liquid egg substitute equal to 2 eggs
¼ cup skim milk
6 1-inch-thick slices French bread
1 to 2 tablespoons powdered or confectioners' sugar

▶ EQUIPMENT

13-by-9-inch baking pan or baking dish
Measuring cups
Small bowl
Fork
Measuring spoons
Glass pie plate
Aluminum foil
Oven mitts
Wire cooling rack

▶ INSTRUCTIONS

1 Place margarine in baking pan or heat-proof baking dish. Place pan on burner. Turn heat to low. Heat margarine until melted.

2 Place brown sugar in small bowl. With fork, stir in cinnamon. Sprinkle mixture evenly over melted margarine in baking pan or dish.

3 Combine egg substitute and milk in glass pie plate. Mix with fork until blended.

4 With fingers or fork, dip bread slices into egg mixture to coat both sides. Lay slices over sugar-cinnamon mixture in baking pan or dish. Pour any remaining egg mixture over the bread slices.

5 Cover pan with foil and refrigerate overnight.

6 Remove pan from refrigerator 1 hour before baking. Let stand on the kitchen counter to reach room temperature.

7 Preheat oven to 375° F.

8 Carefully place pan of French toast in hot oven. Bake 25 minutes.

9 Using oven mitts, remove pan from oven to wire cooling rack. With oven mitts, carefully remove foil from pan.

10 Return pan to hot oven. Bake for 15 minutes longer.

11 Using oven mitts, remove pan to cooling rack. Sprinkle French toast with powdered sugar. Serve warm.

▶ **COOK'S NOTE**

Here's a terrific breakfast treat, but to make it you'll need to think ahead. You need to start this recipe the day before you serve it, since it must be refrigerated over-night. Use crusty loaves of French bread cut into slices. Regular white bread slices won't work—they're too soft and will get soggy.

▶ **COOK'S NOTE**

Egg substitute is available in containers in the dairy section or freezer case of your supermarket. It is lower in cholesterol than eggs and can be used in many recipes. Read the package label to see how much egg substitute is equal to each egg.

▶ **COOK'S NOTE**

When measuring brown sugar, follow these simple steps:
● Spoon the brown sugar out of its box into the correct size dry measuring cup.
● With your hand or the back of a wooden spoon, push the brown sugar into the measuring cup to "pack" it.
● Continue spooning in the sugar and packing it down until the cup is full and level on the top.
● When directed in the recipe to add the brown sugar, turn the cup upside down into the bowl. The sugar should come out easily and hold its "cup" shape.

DESSERTS

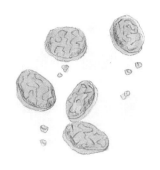

Rosy Cinnamon Applesauce
Tropical Fruit Sherbet
Hidden Treasure Cake
Gingersnaps
Pumpkin Custards à la Mode

Is dessert the part of the meal you look forward to the most? There are lots of people who feel that way. That's why we couldn't think of putting together a cookbook without a dessert chapter.

You'll find a good selection of scrumptious sweets here. But every one of these rich-tasting recipes has been carefully developed to fit into a heart-healthy eating plan. These are desserts with a difference. The fruits, low-fat dairy products, and other ingredients used in these recipes provide vitamins, minerals, and other nutrients as well as great flavor. Even their names will tempt your sweet tooth—Pumpkin Custards à la Mode, Tropical Fruit Sherbet, and Hidden Treasure Cake. Why not whip up all of them for a healthy dessert party?

ROSY CINNAMON APPLESAUCE

Serves 5; ½ cup per serving

Skill Level: **1**

This dessert gets its rosy color from the addition of those small, round cinnamon candies known as "red hots." You can serve this zero-fat applesauce by itself, spoon it over waffles or pancakes, or swirl it into vanilla yogurt.

▶ INGREDIENTS

1 24-ounce jar unsweetened
   applesauce
1 tablespoon cinnamon "red-hot"
   candies
⅛ teaspoon ground cinnamon

▶ EQUIPMENT

Measuring spoons
Medium saucepan
Wooden spoon
Oven mitts

▶ INSTRUCTIONS

1 Combine applesauce, candies, and cinnamon in medium saucepan.

2 Place saucepan on burner. Turn heat to medium.

🖐 **3** Stir applesauce mixture with wooden spoon over medium heat for 3 minutes, or until candies are melted.

4 Using oven mitts, remove saucepan from heat. Place on heatproof surface. Let stand until slightly cooled. Serve applesauce warm, or cover and refrigerate to serve chilled.

TROPICAL FRUIT SHERBET

Serves 4; divided equally

Skill Level: **2**

One lick of frosty, fruity sherbet can make the hottest summer day seem cool as a breeze. And this version couldn't be easier to create. You don't need any fancy equipment like an ice cream maker. Simply whirl the ingredients together in a blender, then freeze the mixture in a baking pan. Open the freezer door a few hours later, and this icy refresher will be ready to scoop.

▶ INGREDIENTS

1 3-ounce package strawberry
    gelatin
½ cup boiling water
1 tablespoon lemon juice
1 20-ounce can pineapple chunks
    in juice, undrained
1 ripe banana
1 10-ounce package frozen,
    sweetened strawberries in
    quick-thaw pouch

▶ EQUIPMENT

Measuring cups
2-cup glass measuring cup
Mixing spoon
Electric blender
Measuring spoons
Can opener
Table knife
11-by-7-inch baking pan or
    individual plastic containers
    (may be an ice-cube tray) with
    wood, paper, or plastic dessert
    sticks (not pointed)

▶ INSTRUCTIONS

1 Combine gelatin and boiling water in glass measuring cup. Stir with mixing spoon until gelatin is dissolved.

2 Pour into electric blender. Add lemon juice and pineapple chunks with their juice. Peel banana and cut into chunks with a table knife. Add to blender.

3 Put lid on blender. Turn on high speed. Blend ingredients until they are liquefied, about 45 seconds. Turn off blender.

4 Remove container from base of blender. Remove lid from blender and pour mixture into baking pan.

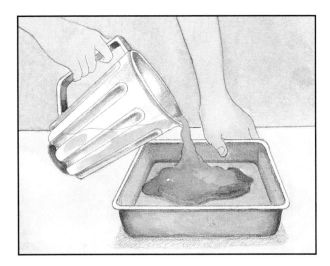

5 Place pan directly on shelf in freezer. Freeze uncovered for 2 to 3 hours, or until mixture is firm.

6 Defrost strawberries in pouch according to package instructions. (This usually takes about 15 to 20 minutes in warm water.)

7 Remove sherbet from freezer 15 minutes before serving to soften slightly. Scoop or spoon sherbet into 4 dessert dishes. Top each serving with ¼ cup strawberries in juice. Serve immediately.

▶ **VARIATION**

You can also use this recipe to make individual tropical fruit pops. Use the same ingredients, except leave off the strawberry topping. Stop after step 3 and pour the blended mixture into individual plastic containers. When almost frozen, place a stick in the middle of each pop. Then freeze until pops are firm (2 to 3 hours).

HIDDEN TREASURE CAKE

Serves 18; 1 slice per serving

Skill Level: **2**

The pieces of fruit that "hide" in this moist cake add lots of good nutrition and natural sweetness. Once it's baked and cooled, the cake can be cut into squares, wrapped in foil or plastic wrap, and frozen in individual pieces. These can then be packed into lunch boxes or brown bags for a sweet surprise.

▶ INGREDIENTS

2 to 3 ripe bananas
⅔ cup (1 stick plus 2⅔ tablespoons)
    margarine
1½ cups sugar
Liquid egg substitute equal to
    3 eggs
¾ cup low-fat buttermilk
1 tablespoon vanilla extract
3 cups all-purpose flour
2 teaspoons baking powder
½ teaspoon salt
1 15-ounce can pineapple tidbits
2 8¼-ounce cans sliced peaches
Vegetable oil spray

▶ GLAZE

⅓ cup fresh lime juice (juice of 1
    large lime)
½ cup sugar

▶ EQUIPMENT

Small, shallow bowl
Fork
Measuring cups
2 medium mixing bowls
Small, sharp knife
Small saucepan or small microwave-safe
    bowl and wax paper
Measuring spoons
Electric mixer
Wire strainer, sieve, or sifter
Rubber spatula
Can opener
13-by-9-inch baking pan
Oven mitts
Wire cooling rack
Small bowl
Table knife
Spoon

▶ INSTRUCTIONS

1 Peel bananas. Place in a small, shallow bowl and mash with a fork. Measure 1 cup mashed bananas into medium mixing bowl.

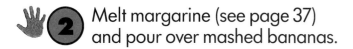

2 Melt margarine (see page 37) and pour over mashed bananas.

3 Add 1½ cups sugar, egg substitute, buttermilk, and vanilla extract to mashed bananas.

4 Place bowl under beaters of electric mixer. Turn mixer on to medium speed. Beat ingredients together for 1 minute.

5 Place strainer, sieve, or sifter over empty medium bowl. Measure flour, baking powder, and salt into strainer, sieve, or sifter. Sift flour mixture into bowl.

6 Add half the sifted flour mixture to banana mixture. Turn electric mixer to low speed. Beat ingredients for 30 seconds. Turn mixer off. Scrape sides of bowl with rubber spatula to push batter back into bowl.

7 Turn mixer back on to low speed. Add remaining flour mixture to batter, stopping mixer after 15 seconds to scrape bowl. Beat for 15 seconds more, or until well mixed.

8 Preheat oven to 350° F.

9 Open can of pineapple tidbits. Empty tidbits into strainer and drain well. Press tidbits lightly with fingertips to squeeze out juice.

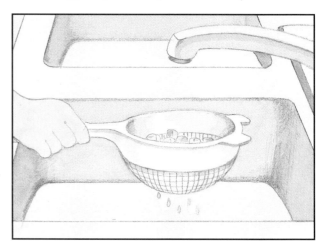

10 Add drained tidbits to cake batter. Mix with rubber spatula until combined. Wash and dry hands.

11 Spray baking pan with vegetable oil spray. Pour cake batter into pan. Spread batter evenly in pan with rubber spatula.

12 Open cans of peaches. Empty peaches into strainer and drain well. Lay peach slices in rows on top of cake batter.

 13 Place pan of batter on middle oven rack. Bake 35 to 40 minutes. Cake is done when table knife inserted in center comes out clean.

 14 Using oven mitts, transfer pan to wire cooling rack.

15 Mix lime juice and ½ cup sugar in a small bowl. Spoon mixture evenly over hot cake.

16 Let cake cool in pan on wire cooling rack at least 45 minutes. To serve, cut into 18 pieces.

▶ **COOK'S NOTE**

One of the most essential parts of baking is measuring the flour correctly. This recipe calls for measuring the flour before sifting. Here's how to do it:
- Lightly stir the flour in its container.
- Spoon the flour into a dry measuring cup. *Do not* dip the measuring cup into the flour.
- Place the cup over a sheet of wax paper. Using a metal spatula or table knife, level off the top, making it flat and even.
- Pour the measured flour into the strainer, sieve, or sifter as directed in the recipe.

GINGERSNAPS

Makes about 5 dozen cookies
Serves 30; 2 cookies per serving

Skill Level: **3**

Many cookie recipes begin by "creaming" together sugar and shortening. Here, margarine is used instead of shortening. If you choose a stick margarine, it can easily be measured by looking at the tablespoon markings on the wrapper and cutting off the amount you need. Each stick equals 8 tablespoons. The margarine and sugar are then combined in a mixing bowl and beaten until a light, fluffy mixture forms. Creaming helps make the cookies moist and delicious.

▶ INGREDIENTS

1¼ sticks (10 tablespoons)
   margarine, at room temperature
1 cup sugar
1 egg
¼ cup molasses
1 teaspoon butter-flavored extract
2 cups sifted all-purpose flour
1¼ to 1½ teaspoons ground ginger
1 teaspoon ground cinnamon
1 teaspoon ground cloves
¼ teaspoon baking soda
¼ cup sugar

▶ EQUIPMENT

Measuring cups
Large mixing bowl
Electric mixer
Rubber spatula
Measuring spoons
Small bowl
2-cup glass measuring cup
Small, metal spatula

Strainer, sieve, or flour sifter
Medium bowl
Plastic wrap
Small, shallow bowl
Cookie sheet
Oven mitts
Pancake turner
Wire cooling rack
Airtight container

▶ INSTRUCTIONS

1 Put margarine and 1 cup sugar in large mixing bowl. Place bowl under beaters of electric mixer. Turn mixer on to medium speed. Beat ingredients until light and fluffy, about 4 to 5 minutes. Stop mixer every now and then and use a rubber spatula to scrape sides of bowl.

2 Break egg into small bowl. Add egg to margarine and sugar mixture. Turn mixer on to low or medium speed. Beat ingredients until well blended. Turn mixer off.

3 Combine molasses and butter-flavored extract in glass measuring cup; set aside.

4 Place strainer, sieve, or flour sifter over empty medium bowl. Measure flour, ginger, cinnamon, cloves, and baking soda into strainer, sieve, or flour sifter. Sift ingredients into bowl.

5 Add half of flour mixture to margarine mixture. Turn mixer on to low speed. Mix ingredients until blended. Turn mixer off.

6 Add molasses mixture; beat on low speed to blend. Turn mixer off.

7 Add remaining flour mixture. Beat on low speed until blended.

8 Cover mixing bowl with plastic wrap and refrigerate dough for 1 hour.

9 Preheat oven to 375° F.

10 Place ¼ cup sugar in small, shallow bowl.

11 Lightly flour hands. With palms of hands, roll dough into 1-inch balls. Roll each ball in sugar. Place 12 balls 2 inches apart on ungreased cookie sheet. Wash and dry hands.

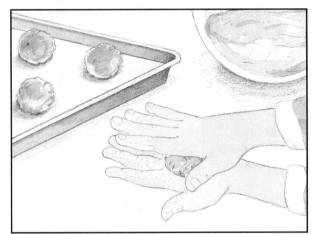

12 Place cookie sheet in oven. Bake cookies for 8 to 10 minutes, or until golden brown.

13 Using oven mitts, remove cookie sheet from oven. Cookies will have cracked tops. Let cookies cool on cookie sheet for 1 minute.

14 Using pancake turner, remove cookies from cookie sheet to wire cooling rack.

15 Allow cookie sheet to cool 15 minutes. Place 12 more balls two inches apart on cooled cookie sheet. Bake as instructed in steps 12–14.

16 Repeat step 15 until all dough has been used.

17 Let cookies cool completely. Store in an airtight container.

▶ **C O O K ' S   N O T E**

For this recipe, measure the flour after it has been sifted. Then sift the flour again with the spices and baking soda as directed in step 4.

▶ **D I D   Y O U   K N O W ?**

Long ago, sugar was considered a luxury item. It was a rare and costly product used mostly by the rich. Less wealthy cooks sweetened their baked goods and desserts with molasses or honey. These days, sugar is used by everybody, but a hint of molasses gives these cookies their unique flavor.

PUMPKIN CUSTARDS À LA MODE

Serves 6; 1 custard per serving

Skill Level: 3

Fans of pumpkin pie know that even though pumpkin is a vegetable, it can make a luscious sweet dessert. But not as many people know about the nutritional value of pumpkin. It's very high in vitamin A and contains no fat or cholesterol. The evaporated skim milk and egg substitute also help keep the cholesterol count down in this recipe, making it a healthy and festive dessert choice. These pumpkin custards would add just the right ending to a Thanksgiving feast or holiday dinner.

▶ INGREDIENTS

1 12-ounce can evaporated
   skim milk
Liquid egg substitute equal to
   4 eggs
⅓ cup sugar
1 16-ounce can pumpkin
1½ teaspoons vanilla extract
½ teaspoon ground cinnamon
½ teaspoon salt
¼ teaspoon ground nutmeg
Vegetable oil spray
5 cups hot water
3 cups vanilla ice milk

▶ EQUIPMENT

Can/bottle opener
Small saucepan or 2-cup
   microwave-safe glass measuring
   cup with handle
Medium mixing bowl
Electric mixer
Measuring cups
Can opener
Rubber spatula

Measuring spoons
6 6-ounce (3½-by-2 inches) ovenproof
   glass custard cups
13- x 9-inch baking pan or baking dish
Table knife
Oven mitts
Wire cooling rack
Scoop

▶ INSTRUCTIONS

1 Preheat oven to 325° F.

2 Using can/bottle opener, open the can of evaporated skim milk and pour into small saucepan. Place saucepan on burner.

Turn heat to medium. Heat milk for 5 minutes, or until hot. Do not boil. Remove from heat.

▶ MICROWAVE INSTRUCTIONS

Pour milk into 2-cup microwave-safe glass measuring cup. Microwave on HIGH (100% power) 3 minutes. Remove from heat and set aside.

3 Pour egg substitute into medium mixing bowl. Place beaters of electric mixer in egg substitute. Turn mixer to medium speed. Beat for 1 minute. Turn off mixer. Add sugar to mixing bowl.

4 Open can of pumpkin. Empty pumpkin into mixing bowl, scraping sides of can clean with rubber spatula.

5 Add vanilla extract, cinnamon, salt, and nutmeg to pumpkin mixture. Beat with mixer on medium speed for 1 minute.

6 Stir in heated evaporated milk and beat 1 minute longer.

7 Spray each custard cup with vegetable oil spray. Place custard cups in baking pan or dish.

8 Pour pumpkin mixture into custard cups, dividing evenly. Pour hot water into baking pan or dish around cups.

9 Carefully place baking pan or dish in preheated oven. Bake custards, uncovered, for 35 minutes, or until a table knife inserted into the middle of a custard comes out clean.

10 Using oven mitts, carefully remove baking pan or dish from oven. Keep oven mitts on while removing custard cups from pan and placing on wire rack to cool.

11 When custards are cooled to room temperature, place in refrigerator. Chill 1 to 2 hours or overnight.

12 To remove each custard from its cup, run a table knife around edge of custard. Carefully tip from cup onto a small dish or plate.

13 To serve, top each custard with a ½-cup scoop of vanilla ice milk. Serve immediately.

▶ **COOK'S NOTE**

When you hear "can opener," you probably think of the kind you use to remove the entire top of a can. The type you use to open a can of milk punctures a hole in the top of the can. After punching holes on opposite sides of the lid, you can pour the milk out easily and neatly.

▶ **COOK'S NOTE**

These pumpkin custards are baked in what is called a "hot water bath." That means hot water is poured into the baking pan or dish around the custard cups to help control the heat and evenly cook the custards. This method will help you turn out custards that are velvety smooth and free of lumps. Be sure an adult helps you with this recipe. The hot water can easily spill and burn you.

BEVERAGES

Three Shakes for Breakfast
Sunset Punch

When you feel like something a little fancier than a glass of juice or milk, try one of these easy-to-make drinks. The shakes could hit the spot at lunch or snacktime as well as breakfast. And the Sunset Punch would add a festive touch to any meal, especially an outdoor barbecue or picnic.

THREE SHAKES FOR BREAKFAST

Serves 1   *Skill Level: 1*

How can you make breakfast in a glass—in a flash? Just pick your favorite fruit, add some milk and cottage cheese, blend in a bit of flavoring and a few ice cubes. Presto—you have a creamy, calcium-rich shake to start the day off right.

SHAKE ONE—BANANA

▶ INGREDIENTS

1 cup skim milk
1 ripe banana, peeled and cut in half
⅓ cup low-fat cottage cheese
1½ teaspoons sugar
1 teaspoon vanilla extract
3 to 4 ice cubes
Dash ground nutmeg

SHAKE TWO—STRAWBERRY-BANANA

▶ INGREDIENTS

1 cup skim milk
½ cup frozen unsweetened whole strawberries
½ ripe banana, peeled and cut in half
⅓ cup low-fat cottage cheese
1 teaspoon vanilla extract
1½ teaspoons sugar
2 ice cubes
2 to 3 drops orange extract

SHAKE THREE—RASPBERRY

▶ INGREDIENTS

1 cup skim milk
⅔ cup frozen unsweetened whole raspberries
⅓ cup low-fat cottage cheese
1 teaspoon vanilla extract
1½ teaspoons sugar
2 ice cubes
2 to 3 drops almond extract

▶ EQUIPMENT

Measuring cups
Measuring spoons
Electric blender
Tall glass

▶ INSTRUCTIONS

1 Place all ingredients for one shake in blender. Cover and turn to high speed. Blend for 45 seconds, or until creamy and smooth.

2 To serve, pour into tall glass.

S U N S E T   P U N C H

Serves 2; approximately ¾ cup per serving   *Skill Level:* **1**

Here's a refreshing drink to sip at sunset, sunrise, or anytime in between. The orange juice should be measured into a clear glass or plastic measuring cup with a pouring spout. A 2-cup or 4-cup size would work best. To measure accurately, set the measuring cup on a flat countertop or table. Then bend down so your eyes are level with the measuring line you need. Slowly pour in the orange juice until it reaches the 1½-cup mark.

▶ I N G R E D I E N T S

1½ cups orange juice
1 tablespoon grenadine syrup
6 to 8 grape ice cubes (see
   Cook's Note below)
2 lime slices

▶ E Q U I P M E N T

Measuring cups
Tall glasses
Measuring spoons

▶ I N S T R U C T I O N S

1 For each serving, pour ¾ cup orange juice into a tall glass. Pour ½ tablespoon grenadine syrup into center of each glass. It will sink to the bottom and create a rosy "sunset" effect.

2 Add 3 to 4 grape ice cubes to each glass.

3 Garnish each glass with a lime slice. Serve immediately.

▶ C O O K ' S   N O T E

To prepare grape ice cubes, you can use regular ice trays or ones with star, heart, bell, or other novelty shapes. Fill trays about halfway full with grape juice (you'll need about 2 tablespoons grape juice for each cube). Freeze about 2 hours, or until solid.

▶ C O O K ' S   N O T E

Grenadine syrup is a non-alcoholic red syrup found in the bar-supply section of your supermarket.

MESSAGE TO PARENTS

Remember when "healthy eating" meant cleaning up everything on your plate and asking for seconds? Those were the days when Mom cooked most of the meals and worried that her children might be malnourished if they didn't eat enough.

Times have certainly changed, and so have many moms. In a number of homes, busy mothers are now sharing the cooking with other family members. And one of our biggest concerns is eating too much—especially when it comes to fat, cholesterol, sodium, and calories.

The Diet-Health Connection

Many studies have indicated that the typical American diet may be linked to a variety of health problems, including obesity, high blood pressure, high blood cholesterol levels, atherosclerosis, and more. Atherosclerosis is the buildup of cholesterol, fatty deposits, and other substances on the inner lining of artery walls, which can narrow the arteries, preventing sufficient blood flow to the heart. This can result in death or damage to part of the heart muscle—a heart attack. There is compelling evidence that this atherosclerotic buildup begins in childhood, and some studies have shown that it can slowly progress into coronary heart disease in adulthood.

Establishing healthy eating habits at an early age may go a long way toward preventing these problems. For example, an elevated blood cholesterol level is an important contributor to atherosclerosis,

and a child's diet can have a significant effect on that level. But how can you help your children make the smartest food choices?

Guidelines for Heart-Smart Eating

Let's start with some general recommendations we've developed for healthy adolescents and children over the age of two.

- Eat a wide variety of foods to get all the nutrients growing bodies need. No single food provides all the essential nutrients in the amounts required. So choosing a variety of foods from all the food groups (see pages 104–105) is the best way to ensure a nutritionally adequate diet.

- Take in enough calories to provide energy for everyday activities and to reach or maintain recommended body weight. Energy or calorie needs depend on a child's height, weight, frame, rate of growth, and level of physical activity. Talk to your doctor or a qualified nutrition counselor about your child's caloric needs. Remember, children who get a lot of exercise use up more energy and require more calories.

- Limit fat intake to an average of no more than 30 percent of total calories. Substitute foods that are low in fat and rich in carbohydrates, such as cereals, grains, fruits, and vegetables, in place of many fatty foods. This recommendation makes it possible for youngsters over the age of two to take in sufficient calories and nutrients for growth and development.

- Since the saturated fat and cholesterol in foods tends to raise blood cholesterol levels, these should be limited too. Limit saturated fat to less than 10 percent of total calories and cholesterol to less than 300 milligrams a day.

A Change in Style

While it's not necessary to hit these figures on the button every day, it might be wise for many families to rethink their eating, cooking, and fitness styles. Begin by eating a lower-fat diet yourself, becoming a positive role model for your children. Then follow through with a specific plan of action. Our "Guidelines for a Low-Fat, Low-Cholesterol Diet" on pages 104–105 are a good starting point. Here's some more healthy "food for thought."

- Fruits, vegetables, and grain products are generally lower in fat and contain no cholesterol. Include these more often in meals and snacks. Try to introduce your children to the exciting selection now available in most supermarkets.

- All animal products contain cholesterol in varying amounts. They are also usually higher in fat (especially the saturated type). But these foods do provide nutrients we all need. To keep fat and cholesterol down and nutritive value up, choose lean meats, skinless poultry, fish, and low-fat or nonfat (skim) dairy products most often.
- Processed foods can be high in fat, cholesterol, and sodium. Share the food shopping with your children and teach them how to read labels on food packages. *Nutrition labels* list the grams of fat and sometimes the milligrams of cholesterol. They also may list the percentage of fat in the product. *Ingredient labels* reveal the types of fat used in processing. Go easy on foods containing tropical oils (coconut, palm, and palm

kernel), cocoa butter, and hydrogenated shortening. These are high in saturated fat even though they don't come from animal sources. The ingredients on the label are listed in order of greatest amount. So the first item on the ingredient list is the one contained in the product in the greatest amount.

- Cook lean and inspire your children to choose recipes that do the same. Try broiling, baking, microwaving, steaming, and poaching, which require little or no fat. Sautéing, stir-frying, and braising require only a small amount of fat. They too are acceptable methods of food preparation.
- Snacking is a natural part of a child's eating style. Munching between meals is one way to get essential nutrients and calories children may not get at breakfast, lunch, and dinner. Healthy snacking is the key. Be sure to stock up on nutritious nibbles. Fresh fruits and vegetables, unbuttered popcorn, rice cakes, toasted sunflower seeds, low-fat cheeses, and dried fruits are all good snack choices. Low-fat and nonfat yogurt are also excellent snacks. Frozen yogurt to which you add fruit is another nutritious treat.

- Keep in mind that small appetites can change from day to day and so can food intake. What's more, a child may offset a high-fat splurge on Monday with healthier eating on Tuesday. Therefore it's best to look at the meals and snacks eaten over a period of several days or even a couple of weeks to see if fat, saturated fat, and cholesterol are in control.

- Physically fit and active children are less likely to be overweight and more likely to have desirable blood cholesterol levels. Organized sports are not the only way to put more exercise into their lives. A brisk walk to school, a family soccer game in the backyard, a bike ride around the neighborhood, or any kind of spontaneous outdoor play can all be beneficial. Try to avoid rigid, overly structured exercise programs. Kids don't usually stick with them. The idea is to get your children moving and have fun. One of the best ways to do this is by joining in yourself!
- Beware of organizing an eating regimen that's too rigid or rigorous. Moderation

is the key to success. Unless your doctor advises otherwise, it's best not to restrict fat intake more than is recommended.

- As a child begins to develop good eating habits, be sure to give him or her praise and encouragement. A child who reaches for unbuttered popcorn instead of potato chips at snack time is making a good choice. So is the child who chooses low-fat milk instead of a thick shake with every meal at the local fast-food spot. You may want to reward a child's all-out effort with an occasional nonedible treat such as a movie pass or tickets to a ball game.
- Don't expect instant results. It's much better to change eating and exercise habits gradually, until they become a way of life.

Ask Dr. Moller

Heart attack is the leading cause of death and illness in our country. The primary goal of the American Heart Association is prevention of cardiovascular disease—the diseases of the heart and blood vessels in the cardiovascular system. For many years, we've known that diet can play an important role in preventing coronary artery disease in adults. Coronary artery disease is a condition that causes narrowing of coronary arteries so blood

flow to the heart muscle is reduced. Only more recently have we discovered that what we eat as children may also affect our future health—particularly when it comes to heart disease. There is now general agreement that atherosclerosis, the accumulation of cholesterol and other substances in the inner lining of the arteries, may begin in youth. This condition can then become progressively more serious as we grow into middle age.

Pediatricians have for many years focused on preventive medicine. Many of us are now turning our attention toward preventing coronary heart disease in children. We are also beginning to control some of the risk factors for this condition, such as high blood cholesterol. We know that high blood cholesterol can be reduced by making small but significant changes in eating habits. We also hope that if these changes are made early, they have a good chance of lasting a lifetime. Toward that end, we've developed a set of dietary recommendations for all healthy children and adolescents over the age of about two years. Each of these recommendations is intended to refer to an average of nutrient intake over a period of several days.

- Nutritional adequacy should be achieved by eating a wide variety of foods.
- Energy (calories) should be adequate to support growth and development and to reach or maintain desirable body weight.
- The following pattern of nutrient intake is recommended:
  — Saturated fatty acids—less than 10 percent of total calories
  — Total fat—an average of no more than 30 percent of total calories
  — Dietary cholesterol—less than 300 mg per day

We've taken some of the work out of translating these figures into actual food choices in our "Guidelines for a Low-Fat, Low-Cholesterol Diet" on pages 104–105. In the Question and Answer section below, we've tried to answer other pressing questions you may have about these recommendations and about diet and health in general. These answers are based on information gathered from the latest scientific studies.

Q. By following your recommendations, will children be eating a nutritionally adequate and balanced diet?

A. Yes. We're simply suggesting modifications in eating habits—not radical changes. We recommend such foods as low-fat dairy products, fish, poultry, lean meats, and plenty of grains, fruits, and vegetables. By choosing these foods, children can take in enough of the high-quality protein they require for growth without taking in too much fat and cholesterol. This eating plan also provides the calcium, vitamins, minerals, and calories that growing, active bodies need. Remember to eat a variety of foods from all the food groups. That's the best way to ensure an adequate diet.

Q. Do overweight children face a greater chance of developing heart disease?

A. Even in children and adolescents, obesity is associated with high blood pressure and increased total blood cholesterol. Both of these, in turn, are risk factors for heart disease. To determine if a child is overweight, consult your pediatrician; he or she will have the most current height-weight tables and methods for gauging excess weight.

Q. To keep a lid on obesity and cholesterol level, wouldn't it be better simply to limit fat and cholesterol intake to a bare minimum?

A. Not at all. Although our bodies produce all of the cholesterol necessary for proper functioning, we do require a small amount of fat from food. Fat performs several roles in the body. For example, it insulates against the cold, helps keep hormones in balance, and aids in absorption of vitamins A, D, E, and K. Limiting dietary fat to a bare minimum can have a negative effect on health and appearance.

Q. What other risk factors play a part in cardiovascular health?

A. There are a few other variables that can affect cardiovascular health, most of which can be controlled. For example, regular physical activity can promote a healthier heart in two ways. It can help keep body weight in a desirable range. It can also increase the level of high density lipoproteins (HDLs)—the so-called good cholesterol. Cigarette smoking, on the other hand, can increase the likelihood of developing atherosclerosis. We need to begin encouraging kids to exercise and discouraging them from smoking early in childhood. These habits may then become a natural part of their lifestyle when they become adults.

Some children with elevated blood cholesterol have inherited the tendency for this condition from their parents. Obviously, heredity is one risk factor that cannot be controlled. But despite this genetic influence, many people with this inherited risk can reduce their cholesterol, often through dietary and lifestyle changes alone. However, in a small percentage of cases, medical intervention might be necessary.

Q. What is a desirable blood cholesterol level for children?

A. An acceptable total cholesterol level for children is less than 170 milligrams per deciliter (mg/dl). Recent studies show that about 15 percent of young Americans between the ages of 4 and 19 have total cholesterol levels that are 200 mg/dl or higher. These children are at high risk for developing heart and blood vessel diseases.

Q. Should cholesterol testing be a routine procedure for all children?

A. We don't recommend cholesterol screening for all children. We do suggest it for children with a family history of heart and blood vessel diseases and children who have a parent with high blood cholesterol.

Q. You've mentioned HDL cholesterol. What does this mean, and how is it related to LDL cholesterol?

A. Cholesterol is carried through the bloodstream in packages called lipoproteins. High-density lipoproteins, or HDLs, are the "good" type that carry cholesterol away from body cells and tissues to the liver for excretion from the body. Low-density lipoproteins, or LDLs, are the "bad" type responsible for depositing cholesterol on artery walls. When a blood sample is evaluated for cholesterol level, the cholesterol reading can be further broken down into HDL and LDL composition. In certain instances, your doctor may want to do this. It's desirable for both children and adults to have high HDL and low LDL cholesterol.

Q. What are triglycerides?

A. Triglycerides are blood fats. Since a high level of these fats is also linked to risk of heart and blood vessel diseases, your doctor may also wish to order a triglyceride reading from a blood sample. This requires a blood sample taken after an overnight fast, whereas a blood cholesterol evaluation does not.

Q. If a child has high levels of blood cholesterol, LDLs, and triglycerides, will he or she have these same high levels as an adult?

A. There is some evidence to suggest that some children with high levels of these substances will be more likely than the general population to have high levels as adults.

Q. What should I do if my child has elevated blood cholesterol?

A. Consult your child's doctor to find out your options. He or she will often recommend nutrition counseling as a first step. You will probably be advised to follow a plan for your child similar to our "Guidelines for a Low-Fat, Low-Cholesterol Diet" on pages 104–105. Your doctor may also suggest a plan for increasing your child's physical activity. Exercise not only has a positive effect on heart health, it can help raise the proportion of good HDLs in the bloodstream.

Parents and children need to work together to make positive changes in their lifestyles. One natural starting point is the kitchen. That is where you can transform all this information into delicious nutritious eating. Look through the mouth-watering recipes (*see pages 15–96*). These will start you and your children on your way to many years of happy, healthy cooking.

James H. Moller, M.D.

Happy, Healthy Cooking

Now let's talk about the tastiest part of this book—the recipes. Our goal was to make healthy cooking fun and rewarding for the whole family. Our professional recipe developers have done just that. They have created delicious, lower-fat versions of the foods children like best—chili, pizza, chips, frozen desserts, pasta, cookies, and the like. Since snacks play a big role in young lives, we've included many that can fit into a heart-healthy eating pattern. We think you will consider these great alternatives to those high-fat frozen dinners, packaged snacks, baked goods, and fast foods that children often grab when hunger strikes. Our idea was to modify—not eliminate—some of the all-time favorite foods of 8- to 12-year olds.

For the next step, each of the recipes was tested for taste and ease of preparation. Meanwhile, our panel made sure every dish passed strict nutrition and safety guidelines. Safe use of the microwave oven was a special concern of ours. We're proud to say that every recipe in these pages received a stamp of approval from our experts.

However, before your children actually start cooking, you should feel confident about their ability to handle different food preparation tasks. We suggest you read through the text sections of this book together and go over the safety tips, cooking terms, descriptions of equipment, and other information. When it's time to tackle the recipes, choose those that best match your child's skill level. To help you out, each recipe has been rated for ease of preparation and clearly marked with this symbol. (Most of the dishes are simple enough for beginning cooks in this age group.) One chef's hat indicates the recipe is easy to prepare. Two chef's hats mean the recipe is slightly more complex, and so on.

Some of the recipes have steps where young children may need some adult help. We have marked those with this symbol. Remember to lend them a hand with sharp knives, food processors, and other equipment designed for older hands. You might consider slicing potatoes or chopping onions ahead of time and presenting younger chefs with a ready-to-use plastic bag filled with the ingredients they might need for a recipe. Finally, we suggest you take a tour of the kitchen with your children and acquaint them with all the "ins and outs" of equipment, utensils, and storage spaces before they embark on their first cooking adventure.

As your children become more proficient cooks, they might be very enthusiastic about sharing their new skills with you. Welcome this as a terrific opportunity to get a little extra help *and* have some fun in the kitchen. You'll soon celebrate healthy cooking and family togetherness.

THE SMART EATER'S GUIDE TO NUTRITION

Do you sometimes feel confused about what foods you should eat? Guess what? You're not alone! Many of us (grown-ups and children alike) find it hard to sort through all the information we hear about nutrition, then use it to make the smartest food choices.

There's a lot of confusion everywhere about what to eat or not eat. But we do know one thing for sure. What and how we eat can help us look healthy and feel good today, tomorrow, and many years from now, *provided* we make healthy eating a life-long habit. In simple words, healthy eating helps make your body and mind healthier.

The Nutrients You Need

The food you eat is broken down into the different *nutrients* it contains as it passes through your body. These nutrients feed trillions of body cells—from your head to your toes. There are more than fifty known nutrients you need to be healthy. These are divided into six basic groups:

WATER:

The nutrient most important to life. Did you know that your body is more than half water! To stay healthy, you need to drink plenty of water, juices, and other beverages.

CARBOHYDRATES:

The major source of energy for powering your body. Starches and sugars are both types of carbohydrates. Starchy foods (potatoes, pasta, bread, etc.) provide valuable vitamins and minerals along with the energy. *Fiber*, which helps move the food through your body and get rid of wastes, is found in many starchy foods, fruits, and vegetables.

FAT:

Another source of energy. Certain types of fat also supply the essential fatty acids the body needs to function properly. We all need some fat in our diet. The trick is not to overdo it. To keep healthy and fit, it's especially important to limit saturated fat and cholesterol. (*See "A Word about Saturated Fat and Cholesterol" on page107.*)

PROTEIN:

The building blocks for your body. The protein in food helps you grow tall and strong. It also helps build and repair all body cells.

VITAMINS:

A group of nutrients that keep the body running smoothly. Some vitamins help your skin stay healthy. Others are important in healing wounds. Examples of vitamins are vitamin A, vitamin C, and niacin.

MINERALS:

Another group of nutrients necessary for health. Some minerals, such as calcium, help build teeth and bones.

Eat a Variety of Foods

All the nutrients work together to make you go, grow, and glow. But no single food contains every nutrient you need. Therefore, eating a *variety* of foods within each food group *every day* is the best plan of action. To make it easy to choose a varied diet, nutritionists at the American Heart Association came up with a simple daily food guide for kids your age (see the box below). It proves that smart eating doesn't have to mean boring choices.

GUIDELINES FOR A LOW-FAT, LOW-CHOLESTEROL DIET FOR PRE-ADOLESCENTS

FOOD GROUP

Vegetables and fruits, fruit juices, vegetable juices

Breads, cereals, and starchy foods

Milk and cheese (to meet calcium requirement)

Meat, poultry, seafood, dried beans and peas, and eggs*

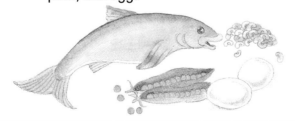

DAILY SERVINGS

4 or more servings
One serving is:
½ cup fruit or vegetable juice
1 medium fruit or vegetable
½ cup cooked or raw fruit or vegetable

4 or more servings
One serving is:
1 slice bread or 1 tortilla
1 cup dry cereal or ½ cup cooked cereal
½ cup cooked pasta, rice, or noodles
2 graham crackers
1 cup popcorn

Minimum of 3 servings
One serving is:
1 8-ounce glass ½ percent or 1 percent milk or low-fat buttermilk
1 ounce low-fat cheese
½ cup low-fat cottage cheese
8 ounces low-fat yogurt

No more than 2 servings daily
One serving is:
2 to 3 ounces cooked lean meat, fish, or poultry
1 cup cooked dried beans or peas

*Egg yolks are limited to 3 to 4 per week; egg whites may be eaten as desired.

Unsaturated fats and oils

Other foods to meet energy needs

4 to 6 servings
One serving is:
1 teaspoon vegetable oil
   or margarine
2 teaspoons diet margarine
2 teaspoons salad dressing,
   mayonnaise, or peanut
   butter
3 teaspoons seeds, nuts,
   chopped avocados,
   or olives

Other low-fat, low-cholesterol
foods to meet energy needs,
or increase portions of above
foods

Staying in Balance

Balance must team up with variety in a healthy eating plan. A balanced diet is one with the right amount of all the nutrients you need in the right proportions. The latest scientific studies show that it's wiser to eat more carbohydrates or starchy foods and less fat. By following the recommended number of servings in the "Guidelines for a Low-Fat, Low-Cholesterol Diet," you'll be doing just that.

All Things in Moderation

The dictionary defines moderation as "controlling excesses." When it comes to eating, that means keeping a watch on foods high in fat, saturated fat, cholesterol, and sodium. This means not going overboard with some of the things you might like best, like hot fudge sundaes and French fries. Don't worry! You won't have to give up these treats completely. Just make sure you eat them less often and balance them with more healthful foods as well. And look for ways to prepare lower-fat versions of your favorites. You'll find recipes for some of them in this book. Do you like chips and dip? Try Tortilla Crisps with Mexi Dip Olé. How about chicken nuggets? Our Shake-It-Up Chicken Nuggets are sure to please. Cornbread fans will like our Cheesy Cornbread. We have also included a chart on page 106 to show how to substitute some ingredients to make your own favorite recipes more heart healthful.

Moderation also means not loading up your plate with more food than your body needs. Food is the fuel that your body burns to make energy. This energy is measured in *calories*. You use up a certain number of calories in everyday activities. What you don't use up is stored on your body as fat. So it's best to take in enough calories to keep your body growing normally without adding too much extra padding. Your doctor can tell you how many calories your developing body needs.

Remember—some foods deliver more nutrients than others and make "better" choices. But there's room for everything in your eating future—in moderation.

Exercise: The Other Half of the Health Equation

You need more than a balanced diet to be healthy. Exercise is also important. The key to a fit, trim body is simple. Balance the food you take in with the energy you use up. Almost any physical activity will burn up extra calories. Exercise is good for your heart too! Try walking, biking, skating, fast dancing, or jumping rope. These are all heart-healthy activities.

Snacks Are Okay

The breakfast-lunch-dinner routine is not the only way to get all your nutrients and calories. In fact, you may find it more convenient to eat smaller meals and enjoy nutritious nibbles in between. Try to choose most of your snacks from the foods suggested in "Guidelines for a Low-Fat, Low-Cholesterol Diet." You'll also find some delicious snack recipes on pages 15–21.

SUBSTITUTION LIST

WHEN YOUR OWN RECIPE CALLS FOR:	USE:
Whole milk (1 cup)	1 cup of skim or nonfat milk plus 1 tablespoon of unsaturated oil.
Heavy cream (1 cup)	1 cup evaporated skim milk or ½ cup low-fat yogurt and ½ cup low-fat cottage cheese.
Sour cream	Low-fat cottage cheese plus low-fat yogurt for flavor; ricotta cheese made from partially skimmed milk (thinned with yogurt or buttermilk, if desired); 1 can of chilled evaporated skim milk whipped with 1 teaspoon of lemon juice; or low-fat buttermilk or low-fat yogurt.
Cream cheese	4 tablespoons of margarine blended with 1 cup dry low-fat cottage cheese. Add a small amount of skim milk if needed in blending the mixture. Add chopped chives or pimiento and herbs and seasonings for variety.
Butter (1 tablespoon)	1 tablespoon polyunsaturated margarine or ¾ tablespoon polyunsaturated oil.
Shortening (1 cup)	2 sticks polyunsaturated margarine.
Oil (1 cup)	1¼ cups polyunsaturated margarine.
Eggs (1 egg)	1 egg white plus 2 teaspoons of unsaturated oil or commercially produced cholesterol-free egg substitute according to package directions. 3 egg whites for 2 whole eggs; 2 egg whites for 1 whole egg in baking recipes.
Unsweetened baking chocolate (1 ounce)	3 tablespoons unsweetened cocoa powder or carob powder plus 1 tablespoon of polyunsaturated oil or margarine. (Carob is sweeter than cocoa, so also reduce sugar in the recipe by one-fourth.)

A WORD ABOUT SATURATED FAT AND CHOLESTEROL

You've heard the words "saturated fat" and "cholesterol" many times. What do they mean?

There are three types of fat—saturated, monounsaturated, and polyunsaturated. Foods contain different amounts of each. Of these three, *saturated fat* can raise the cholesterol level in your blood. A high blood cholesterol level increases the risk of heart disease. Foods high in saturated fat include butter, red meat, ice cream, cream, and whole milk and cheese. Some vegetable oils, such as coconut, palm kernel, and palm oil, are also saturated. *Cholesterol* in foods can also raise your blood cholesterol. Only foods from animal sources contain cholesterol. Eggs, meats, poultry, fish, and dairy products all have varying amounts of cholesterol.

CHOOSING RECIPES AND MAKING MENUS

When you hear the word "menu" you might think of the printed card you order from in a restaurant. But a menu can also be the foods you eat together at one meal. For example, if you're planning to cook Spicy Buttons and Bows for dinner, you might also think about what to serve with it. It's especially handy to have a menu plan in mind when you're putting together a shopping list for ingredients. By considering the entire meal at once, you'll be able to make a healthier menu *and* save time and money as well.

Do you remember variety and balance? They work as well in making menus as they did in choosing a nutritious diet:

- Try to include foods from the different food groups in your menu. For example, you can balance Grandpa's Favorite Soup with crusty bread, a fruit dessert, and a glass of milk. Along with the Spicy Buttons and Bows, you might serve a side dish of steamed broccoli, with frozen yogurt for a sweet ending. Keep in mind that many recipes (like the Polka Dot Chicken Pasta Salad) combine two or more food groups in one dish.
- When you're just learning to cook, you might want to choose the easiest recipes in the book. They are the ones with one chef's hat. As you become more of an expert, try the recipes that have two or three chef's hats.
- Combine different colors and textures for your meal. A plate filled with baked flounder, white rice, and cauliflower could look and taste pretty dull. But team the flounder with a crisp green salad and spaghetti with tomato sauce, and you have a dynamite meal.

- Pick recipes with a variety of flavors that complement each other but don't clash. A spicy Mexican chili wouldn't go too well with Chinese vegetables stir-fried with ginger. But pair the chili with Cheesy Cornbread, and it's a winner!
- When selecting recipes, take a look at the number of servings. If you want to make a meal that serves 4 and the recipe serves 2, you can simply double the recipe. A grown-up can help you figure out how to adjust the recipe to fit the number of people you are serving.
- Contrast hot and cold foods in the same meal. A cool fruit salad is the perfect partner for a hot meatball sub.
- A recipe that takes a lot of time and effort should be the star of your menu. Balance it with foods that need little or no preparation, such as store-bought bread, fresh fruit, store-bought dessert, and a simple beverage.
- Once you've selected a recipe and menu plan, check to see which ingredients you already have on hand. Then make a list of the items you'll need to get at the supermarket. It would also be a good idea to check with a grown-up to make sure you have all the kitchen equipment you need.

Menus

We put together a few menus to help get you started. Each item on the menu is from this book.

You can prepare some of these items in advance. For example, when fixing "Dinner with Friends," you can prepare the salad and dessert early in the day. A few hours before dinner, you can get the chicken ready to go in the oven. That way you'll have less to prepare at dinner time. That means more time to spend with your friends.

You'll want to add a beverage such as skim or low-fat milk to the menus where no beverage is listed.

Remember, these are just suggestions. Use them along with our "Guidelines for a Low-Fat, Low-Cholesterol Diet" on pages 104–105 to make your own menus. You'll soon see that part of the fun of cooking is planning the menu.

DINNER WITH FRIENDS
Shake-It-Up Chicken Nuggets
Speckled Rice
Festive Peas
Shimmering Fruit Salad
Gingersnaps

SATURDAY NIGHT SUPPER
Tasty Turkey Chili
Sunshine Slaw
Rosy Cinnamon Applesauce

COME FOR LUNCH
Garden Patch Soup
Nutty Pineapple Nibbles
Cinnamon Raisin Scones

SURPRISE MOM!
Microwave Lemon Fish
Nutty Broccoli Flowers
Cheesy Cornbread
Pumpkin Custards à la Mode

HOW ABOUT A PARTY?
Pop Snack
Top Hat Pizzas
Hidden Treasure Cake
Sunset Punch

A TRIP THROUGH THE SUPERMARKET

Now that you've chosen your menu plan, it's time to head for the supermarket. Shopping for food can be as confusing as choosing a healthy diet. Just think: the average supermarket has more than 30,000 items! How can you make the smartest choices when you're faced with so many cans, jars, and packages of food?

Let's begin by pushing an imaginary cart down the supermarket aisles. We're going to toss in those foods that deliver the most nutrition without too much fat, saturated fat, cholesterol, or sodium. The major source of sodium in our diet is salt. Once you get the hang of healthy shopping, you'll be ready for a *real* trip to the supermarket. Take a grown-up along and show him or her how much you've learned!

The Produce Department

Fresh fruits and vegetables are a nutritious all-around choice. Most have little or no fat and no cholesterol, and they are packed with vitamins and minerals. Avocados and coconuts are both high in fat. But avocados have primarily mono-unsaturated fat.

Supermarket salad bars offer cut-up vegetables and fruits that are handy to use. Most choices on a salad bar have little or no fat. The few high-fat items you may find are garnishes (bacon bits, chopped nuts, olives), the salad mixtures (potato, macaroni, coleslaw), and some of the creamy dressings.

The Bread/Cereal/Grains Shelves

These are terrific high-energy foods, but you have to look out for hidden fat and sugar at times. Sort out the most healthful choices with the following tips.

CHOOSE MOST OFTEN:
- Whole-grain breads (whole-wheat, oatmeal, cracked wheat)
- Bagels
- English muffins
- Pita bread
- Pumpernickel or rye bread
- Breadsticks
- Tortillas (corn)
- Oatmeal
- Unsweetened ready-to-eat cereals
- Plain rice and pasta

CHOOSE LEAST OFTEN:
- Biscuits
- Sweet muffins
- Croissants
- Doughnuts
- Pastries
- Presweetened cereals
- Granola cereal
- Pasta and rice mixes with sauces and/or seasonings

The Meat, Poultry, and Fish Counter

Meat, poultry, and fish offer high-quality protein, but all contain some saturated fat and cholesterol. Nevertheless, some types contain much less fat than others. Most fish is low in fat. If you need help identifying the cuts listed here, ask the butcher or meat manager to help you. Always select the meats with the least amount of visible fat.

CHOOSE MOST OFTEN:
- Skinless turkey and chicken breasts
- Ground chicken or turkey without skin
- Beef (sirloin, round, loin, or flank)
- Lamb (leg or loin)
- Ground round
- Pork (tenderloin, center loin)
- Sliced cooked turkey or boiled ham
- Fish fillets or steaks
- Shellfish
- Tuna packed in water

CHOOSE LEAST OFTEN:
- Turkey or chicken thighs or drumsticks with skin
- Regular ground beef
- Sausages or hot dogs
- Pork spareribs
- Luncheon meats (salami, bologna, liverwurst)
- Tuna packed in oil
- Breaded fish sticks or fillets
- Seafood entrees prepared with sauces

The Dairy Case

Milk, cheese, and other dairy foods are chock full of calcium—a must for strong bones and teeth. To keep saturated fat and cholesterol down, steer away from dairy products made with whole milk or cream.

CHOOSE MOST OFTEN:
- Skim or low-fat milk (½ or 1 percent fat; or 99 percent or 99.5 percent fat-free)
- Low-fat buttermilk
- Skim-milk or low-fat cheeses that have no more than 5 grams of fat per ounce (check the label)
- Low-fat ricotta and cottage cheese
- Nonfat or low-fat yogurt
- Margarine with no more than 2 grams of saturated fat per tablespoon (check the label)

CHOOSE LEAST OFTEN:
- Whole milk
- Whipping cream or heavy cream
- Light cream or half-and-half
- Cream cheese
- Processed cheese spreads
- Whole-milk cheeses
- Whole-milk yogurt
- Butter

The Frozen Food Case

Select the most simply prepared foods. Those that have been breaded, fried, or covered with sauces or gravies are going to be higher in fat, cholesterol, and salt.

CHOOSE MOST OFTEN:
- Frozen whole-grain waffles
- Plain cheese or vegetarian pizza
- Plain frozen vegetables
- Ice milk or frozen yogurt
- Fruit sherbet or ices

CHOOSE LEAST OFTEN:
- Frozen French fries
- Pepperoni or sausage pizza
- Frozen vegetables with seasoning or sauce packets
- Fried or breaded chicken or fish
- Ice cream

The Snack Food Aisle

Homemade snacks are the best-tasting and most healthful, but sometimes it's hard to resist a bag of munchies.

CHOOSE MOST OFTEN:
- Unsalted, unbuttered popcorn
- Unsalted pretzels
- Whole-wheat or plain crackers
- Oatmeal cookies
- Gingersnaps
- Fruit-filled cookies
- Animal crackers
- Graham crackers
- Unsalted, dry-roasted peanuts

CHOOSE LEAST OFTEN:
- Potato chips
- Corn chips
- Seasoned tortilla chips
- Buttery salted crackers
- Cookies (with the exception of those listed above)
- Frosted cupcakes

A Look at Labels

As you toss your groceries into the shopping cart, you'll notice that many packaged foods now have labels that list nutrition information and ingredients. These labels can be very helpful in choosing the most healthful foods—*if* you know how to read the language. Here are some clues to help you figure out exactly what these labels are telling you.

The Ingredient Label

Most packaged foods contain more than one ingredient. By law, food manufacturers must list these ingredients on the package in order of their weight in the product. For example, if sugar is listed first on a cereal box label, that means the cereal has more sugar than any other ingredient. Also look to see if several sugars (such as sucrose, dextrose, honey, and corn syrup) are listed on the label. That cereal also has a great deal of sugar in it. A better cereal choice is one that lists oats or wheat as the first ingredient.

A product that has "oil" or "butter" near the top of its list is not the most healthful choice either. A bag of chips, for instance, might list "vegetable oil" as its number one ingredient.

Some of the oils and fats used in making food products can also be the less desirable saturated kind, even though the label doesn't come right out and say so. The list of saturated fats below shows some of the names saturated fat hides under on ingredient labels.

SATURATED FATS

Coconut oil
Palm or palm kernel oil
Lard
Hydrogenated shortening
Cocoa butter
Butter
Vegetable oil that is not identified by a specific name on an ingredient list

Healthier choices would be those products made with one of the unsaturated fats listed below.

UNSATURATED FATS

Sunflower oil	Canola oil
Safflower oil	Olive oil
Peanut oil	Corn oil
Cottonseed oil	Soybean oil

The Nutrition Label

A new law has been passed that will soon require all packaged foods to have nutrition labels (*see illustration on this page*). This is what you *will* see:

- The serving size and number of servings per package;
- The number of calories in one serving;
- The amount in grams of protein, carbohydrate, fat, and saturated fat in one serving;
- The amount in milligrams (mg) of sodium in one serving;
- The amount in milligrams (mg) of cholesterol in one serving;
- The recommended Daily Values for the nutrients mentioned above and for calcium, iron, vitamin A, and vitamin C.

Nutrition Facts

Serving Size ½ cup (114g)
Servings Per Container 4

Amount Per Serving

Calories 90   Calories from Fat 30

	% Daily Value*
Total Fat 3g	5%
Saturated Fat 0g	0%
Cholesterol 0mg	0%
Sodium 300mg	13%
Total Carbohydrate 13g	4%
Dietary Fiber 3g	12%
Sugars 3g	
Protein 3g	

Vitamin A	80%	•	Vitamin C	60%
Calcium	4%	•	Iron	4%

* Percent Daily Values are based on a 2,000 calorie diet. Your daily values may be higher or lower depending on your calorie needs:

		Calories	2,000	2,500
Total Fat	Less than		65g	80g
Sat Fat	Less than		20g	25g
Cholesterol	Less than		300mg	300mg
Sodium	Less than		2,400mg	2,400mg
Total Carbohydrate			300g	375g
Fiber			25g	30g

Calories per gram:
Fat 9   •   Carbohydrate 4   •   Protein 4

The best way to use this information is in comparing one product with another. Be sure to compare similar serving sizes. For example, if one package of cheese contains 3 grams of fat per one-ounce slice and another contains 6, the first would be a leaner choice. You can make the same comparisons for calories and other listed nutrients. To help you compare the nutrient values of some of your favorite foods, you may want to look them up in the American Heart Association *Fat and Cholesterol Counter*. If you choose a high-fat or high-cholesterol food, balance it with lower-fat and lower-cholesterol choices for the rest of your meals that day.

The Daily Values are set by the government to help assure that all Americans are properly nourished. These figures are used mostly by dietitians and scientists. However, they can be helpful to you in finding foods that are good sources of certain nutrients. For example, if a container of yogurt lists "35" next to calcium, you know that one serving will provide 35 percent of your daily calcium requirement. That's more than one-third!

Nutrition Claims

Key words and health claims appear on many product labels. When the new law takes effect, you can rest assured that these terms mean what they say as defined by the government. For example:

- "Fat free" means less than 0.5 gram of fat per serving.
- "Low-fat" means 3 grams of fat or less per serving.
- "Lean" means less than 10 grams of fat, 4 grams of saturated fat, and 95 milligrams of cholesterol per serving.
- "Light" or "lite" means a third less calories or no more than half the fat of the higher-calorie, higher-fat version; or no more than half the sodium of the higher-sodium version.
- "Cholesterol free" means less than 2 milligrams of cholesterol and 2 grams or less of saturated fat per serving.

There's a lot of useful information out there on the shelves of your supermarket. But sometimes you've got to do a little detective work to uncover all the nutrition clues!

SETTING THE TABLE

Whether you've cooked a snack, a family meal, or party food, it's nice to serve it on a table that's set properly and looks inviting. You can just do a simple table setting or go all out—the basics are the same for both. And remember—this is an easy job that's good to teach to little brothers and sisters eager to help.

- To set the table, you'll need dinnerware (dishes), glassware, flatware (forks, spoons, and knives), and napkins. In some homes, placemats or tablecloths are also used.
- Use items that will match the meal or food you're serving. For a speedy snack, a paper plate and a paper napkin do just fine. For a home-cooked dinner, you really should use sturdy, attractive dishes that will show off your meal. Party food,

on the other hand, can go on anything from colorful paper plates to the family's best dinnerware. You may decide to use fancy paper napkins or elegant cloth napkins to add the right touch. It's a wise idea to ask a grown-up for help in choosing the most appropriate dishes and utensils the first few times around.

- The steps in setting the table are pretty much the same for any sit-down meal:
  1. Put down the correct number of place mats or the tablecloth, if these are being used.
  2. Arrange the *place setting* on top. A place setting is made up of all the items each person needs for eating.
  3. The *plate* goes in the center of the place setting. The *fork* goes to the left of the plate, with the tines pointing up.

The *napkin* can go under the fork or to the left of it. The napkin can also go on top of the plate. The *knife* is placed to the right of the plate, with its sharp side pointing in. The *spoon* is set next to the knife, and the beverage *glass* goes above the tip of the knife.

4. If more flatware is needed, place it in the order in which it will be used, from the outside in. (If you're ever faced with a lot of forks and spoons at a dinner table, you'll know what to do. Use the ones farthest from your plate first.) (See *illustration*.)

5. If several dishes or courses are served at one meal, you may need extra dishes, such as a small salad plate or bowl or bread and butter plate. The extra dish goes to the left and slightly

above the fork or napkin. A cup and saucer for hot beverages should go to the right of the spoon. (See *illustration*.)

- If there's room, serving utensils and dishes can be placed in the center of the table or on a nearby counter or server. Every family has its own eating style. Some families like to serve themselves from large platters or bowls of food at the table. Others go right up and help themselves from pots and pans on the stove. Sometimes, the cook fills each individual plate with a little of each food and brings it to the table. There really is no right or wrong way to serve a meal. The main goal is to feel comfortable, enjoy the food, and come away from the table well-fed!

CLEANING UP

Your family will be proud of all the things you've already learned about nutrition, food shopping, cooking, and safety. To keep them smiling, make sure you don't forget about cleaning up! It's the cook's job to leave the kitchen in tip-top shape. Here's how to do a great job with the least effort.

- "Clean up as you go along" is the number one rule. It will save you time and energy in the long run.
- Put ingredients away as soon as you finish with them. It's especially important to put refrigerated foods back into the

refrigerator as soon as possible to prevent spoilage.

- Wipe up spills on countertops and floor immediately after they happen. (This speedy action will help prevent accidents too!) Keep sponges and a roll of paper towels handy for these quick clean-ups.
- Always use clean sponges and dishcloths. If you use one sponge for wiping the floor, keep a separate sponge on hand for countertops, dishes, and other jobs.
- Unplug a portable electrical appliance

as soon as you're finished with it. Then wipe it off with a damp cloth or sponge and put it away.

- Rinse off dishes with warm water before loading them into the dishwasher. If you're washing the dishes by hand, soak them first in a sink filled with hot soapy water until you're ready to wash them.
- Soak dirty utensils, pots, and pans in hot soapy water to make the final cleaning easier. (Remember the rule about sharp knives: Put them aside to wash separately.) When ready to wash knives, keep the sharp side turned away from your body. The same goes for drying knives!
- Thoroughly clean cutting boards and other surfaces touched by meat, poultry, or fish. Use hot, soapy water and a scour-

ing pad, if necessary. Then rinse the surfaces thoroughly.

- Throw all food waste into a garbage bag and tie it securely.
- Place leftover cooked food in sealed plastic bags or plastic containers with lids. Or wrap leftovers tightly in aluminum foil or plastic wrap. Store in the refrigerator.
- Let the stove cool before wiping off any spillovers. Then wipe off the countertops, stovetop, and any other work surfaces with a damp sponge or cloth.
- Before you leave the kitchen, make sure the appliances you used are turned off. Also, check the sink once more to make sure the dishes are all done. Then give the sink a quick rinse and turn off the lights!

COOK'S CHATTER

(A Glossary of Cooking Terms, Tools, and Ingredients)

You don't need to have a lot of gadgets to become a smart cook. But getting to know these basic pieces of equipment and cooking terms will make it much easier to follow recipe directions and turn out delicious food.

Kitchen Tools and Descriptive Terms

BAKING SHEET OR JELLY-ROLL PAN: A shallow, rectangular pan that usually measures about 15 by 10 inches. A baking sheet is used for baking bar cookies, thin cakes, and other items.

BLENDER: A small electrical appliance with a tall container that sits on a motorized base. The motor moves a set of sharp blades that can chop, blend, and liquefy ingredients very quickly.

CAN OPENER: A tool with sharp, strong cutting blades designed to pierce and open cans. A can opener can be electric, hand-held, or mounted on the wall.

CASSEROLE: A round, square, or rectangular baking dish made of ceramic, glass, or other heatproof material. A casserole comes in small, medium, and large sizes, and usually has a cover.

COLANDER: A plastic or metal utensil shaped like a bowl and punched with holes. A colander is used for draining pasta, vegetables, and other foods.

COOKIE SHEET: A flat, rectangular metal pan

that's usually open on at least one side. A cookie sheet is used for baking cookies or rolls.

CUSTARD CUPS: Small, heatproof cups usually used for baking custards. These come in sizes ranging from 4 to 10 ounces.

CUTTING BOARD: A thick wooden or plastic slab used for slicing and chopping food. It also keeps countertops from getting scratched!

DUTCH OVEN: A 5- to 8-quart pot with deep sides,  two side handles, and a cover. Soups, stews, chili, and similar dishes are cooked in a Dutch oven.

ELECTRIC MIXER: A piece of equipment used for mixing, whipping, beating, and blending ingredients. A *portable mixer* is a small, hand-held appliance with the beaters attached to a lightweight case. A *stand mixer* is a heavier, more powerful appliance. The beaters are attached to a permanent stand, and the mixing bowl sits on a turntable. When using a stand mixer, be sure to use the mixing bowls designed for that appliance.

FOOD PROCESSOR: A heavy-duty appliance that can perform many time-consuming jobs fast. A food processor has a motorized base, a plastic bowl or container that sits on top, and a cover with an opening to feed in the ingredients. The different types of blades that fit into the container make it possible to chop, shred, grind, and mix food in record time.

GRATER OR SHREDDER: A flat or four-sided metal gadget with sharp-edged openings of different sizes. A grater or shredder is used to grate or shred cheese, carrots, and other foods into fine or coarse pieces.

KITCHEN SCISSORS OR SHEARS: A utensil used for cutting green onions, parsley, bread dough, and various other foods. *Poultry shears* are stronger and sturdier. They are used to cut whole chickens into parts.

KNIVES: Available in several sizes and styles, these are used to slice or cut foods. The most common ones are a 3- or 4-inch paring knife, a 5-inch slicing knife, an 8-inch chef's knife, and a 9-inch carving knife. A *serrated knife* has a wavy or saw-toothed edge. A long one is used for slicing bread, while the smaller sizes are for cutting tomatoes and citrus fruits.

LADLE: A long-handled metal utensil with a small bowl on the end. A ladle is used to scoop foods like soups and stews from the cooking pot.

MEASURING CUPS: These come in two styles—liquid and dry. A *liquid measuring cup* is made of clear glass or plastic marked with lines that measure 1 or more cups or parts of a cup and is used to measure liquids. *Dry measuring cups* are made of metal or plastic and come in a set that includes 1/4-, 1/3-, 1/2-, and 1-cup sizes. They usually nest one inside the other and are used to measure flour, sugar, and other dry ingredients. Both types of measuring cups now come with standard and metric measurements. This book uses standard measurements.

MEASURING SPOONS: These come in metal or plastic sets that are "nested" like the measuring cups. Most sets include spoons ranging from 1/8 teaspoon to 1 tablespoon. They can measure both liquid and dry ingredients.

MICROWAVE-SAFE OR MICROWAVEABLE: Cookware or bakeware that can be used in the microwave oven. These utensils are usually made of plastic, ceramic, glass, or heavy coated paper. Some are made of special materials designed especially for use in the microwave. Metal or metal-containing utensils can *never* be used in the microwave.

MIXING BOWLS: Small, medium, and large bowls used for mixing ingredients. Mixing bowls can be made of metal, plastic, ceramic, or glass. They're often available in sets of two or three.

MIXING SPOONS: Long-handled spoons made of wood, plastic, or metal. They're used to combine ingredients by stirring or mixing.

MUFFIN PAN OR MUFFIN TIN: A metal pan containing individual cups. Muffin pans come with small, medium, or large cups with 6 or 12 cups each. They're used for baking muffins and cupcakes.

NONSTICK: A coating or finish on cookware or bakeware that prevents food from sticking.

OVEN MITTS OR POTHOLDERS: Heatproof pads used to protect the hands, when taking hot dishes from the oven or microwave. They are also used to hold the handle of a saucepan while stirring the hot contents.

OVENPROOF: A cooking or baking utensil that can withstand high heat and temperature changes. It can usually go from the oven to the table.

PARER OR PEELER: A small metal utensil used to remove the thin outer layer of vegetables and fruits.

PIE PLATE: An 8- or 9-inch round metal or glass pan with sloping sides used for baking pies.

PIZZA CUTTER: A utensil with a round metal wheel on top and a wooden or metal handle. The sharp wheel easily cuts through pizza, doughs, and other bread products.

RECTANGULAR BAKING PAN: A 13-by-9-inch or 12-by-8-inch pan used for roasting or for baking bar cookies and sheet cakes.

ROLLING PIN: A heavy wood cylinder-shaped tool with two handles. A rolling pin is used for rolling out dough and pastry and for crushing crackers into crumbs.

SAUCEPAN: A deep, round pot with one long handle on the side. Saucepans come in several sizes, ranging from 1 to 5 quarts. Some recipes call for a "small," "medium," or "large" saucepan instead of a certain size.

SIFTER: A metal utensil containing a wire mesh insert. Flour is measured into the wire mesh and sifted through.

SKILLET OR FRYING PAN: A wide, shallow pan that comes in sizes ranging from 6 to 14 inches. Most recipes call for a "small," "medium," or "large" skillet rather than a certain size.

SPATULA: These come in two styles—metal and rubber. A *metal spatula* has a long, narrow metal blade with dull edges. The blade is flexible enough to frost cakes. A metal spatula is also used to level off ingredients when measuring and to loosen baked cookies and cakes from their pans. A *rubber spatula* has a rubber blade and a wooden or plastic handle. It's used to scrape out and clean the sides of cans, bowls, pans, and the food processor. It is also good for folding batters and ingredients. (See also "turner," this page.)

STRAINER OR SIEVE: A bowl-shaped basket made of metal mesh and attached to a long handle. The tiny holes in the strainer make it possible to separate liquids from solids.

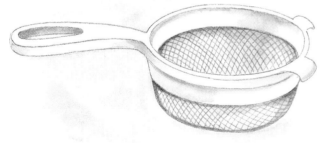

TIMER: A convenient gadget to measure cooking or baking time. Most timers can be set up to 60 minutes, but a few go higher. A timer will ring, beep, or give off another signal when the time is up.

TONGS: A wooden or metal utensil with long arms that can grip foods easily. Tongs are used for turning foods such as meat during cooking, or removing corn or potatoes from boiling water.

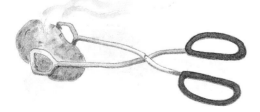

TURNER: Also called a pancake turner, this is a wide spatula with a long handle. A turner is used to flip pancakes, hamburgers, and other foods so both sides are cooked evenly.

VEGETABLE BRUSH: A stiff brush used to scrub clean such vegetables as potatoes and carrots.

WIRE COOLING RACK: A round or rectangular rack used for cooling muffins, breads, cookies, and other baked goods after they come out of the oven.

WIRE WHISK: A metal utensil with a long handle and balloon-shaped top. Available in several sizes, a whisk is used to blend or beat ingredients or to whip egg whites.

WOK: A large, round pan with sloping sides. A wok is used for stir-frying and for Oriental-style dishes.

Cooking Terms

BAKE: To cook by dry heat in the oven.

BEAT: To make a mixture light and smooth with a beater, wire whisk, or electric mixer.

BLEND: To completely mix together two or more ingredients. You may use a fork, whisk, or blender.

BOIL: To cook a liquid over high heat until large bubbles form and break on the surface.

BRAISE: To cook food in a small amount of flavored liquid. Meats and chicken are often braised.

BROIL: To cook by direct heat on a rack under a broiler. This can be done in an oven broiler or a portable toaster-oven broiler.

CHOP: To cut into small, irregular pieces.

COAT: To cover the surface of food or a utensil with vegetable oil spray, flour, crumbs, or other ingredients.

COMBINE: To mix ingredients together thoroughly.

CUBE: To cut food into pieces of the same size and shape.

DICE: To cut into very small pieces of the same square shape and size.

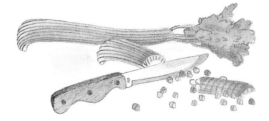

FOLD: To gently combine a delicate mixture with a heavier one. A whisk or rubber spatula is usually used in an over-and-under motion.

FRY: To cook in an open skillet or frying pan in hot oil or other melted fat.

GARNISH: To decorate food by adding a small  amount of a colorful or savory topping. Lemon wedges, parsley sprigs, mint leaves, and other foods are used as garnishes.

GRATE: To cut into very fine shreds or pieces using a hand grater or food processor.

GREASE: To cover the surface of a pan with a thin layer of fat such as margarine, oil, or vegetable oil spray. This prevents food from sticking.

GRILL: To cook over hot coals on a slotted grate that allows the fat to drain away.

GRIND: To chop food very, very finely by forcing it through a grinder or placing it in a blender or food processor.

KNEAD: To work dough with hands until it becomes smooth and stretchy. This is usually done on a floured surface by pressing, turning, and squeezing the dough.

MELT: To heat a solid substance until it becomes liquid. This can be done in a saucepan or microwave oven.

MINCE: To cut or chop such foods as garlic, onions, and parsley into very tiny pieces. You can use a sharp knife, an electric blender, or a food processor to mince foods.

MIX: To combine two or more ingredients until well blended.

PARE: To remove the skin or peel of a fruit or vegetable.

POACH: To cook food in barely boiling water. Fish and eggs are commonly poached.

ROAST: To cook meat or poultry with hot, dry air in the oven or on an outdoor grill.

SAUTÉ: To cook food quickly in an open skillet or frying pan using a small amount of fat. The food should be stirred or turned often.

SHRED: To cut into thin, irregular strips with a knife, shredder, or food processor.

SIFT: To pass flour or other dry ingredients through a sieve or sifter before measuring.

SIMMER: To cook just below the boiling point. The liquid should be bubbling very gently.

STEAM: To cook food in a metal basket set over boiling water.

STEW: To simmer cut-up food for a long time in a small amount of liquid.

STIR-FRY: To cook cut-up food in a small amount of very hot fat over high heat. The food should be lifted and stirred constantly as it cooks.

TOSS: To mix ingredients lightly with a lifting motion. Salads and pasta are usually tossed.

WHIP: To beat rapidly with a wire whisk or electric mixer. Whipping adds air to a mixture and makes it light and fluffy.

Ingredient Terms

APPLES: *Cooking apples* are firm, crisp apples that hold their shape in baking. *Eating apples* are tender and not tart enough for cooking.

BROTH: The liquid base for soups and sauces. Also called stock, broth can be canned or homemade using chicken, beef, or vegetables.

EGG SUBSTITUTE: A liquid replacement for fresh eggs, available frozen or in the refrigerator case. Egg substitutes contain little or no cholesterol.

EVAPORATED SKIM MILK: A canned milk in which half the moisture has been removed, making it thicker than regular skim milk and easy to whip.

HERBS: The fresh or dried leaves of plants that add flavor to cooking.

ICE MILK: A frozen dessert similar to ice cream but with reduced fat and sugar.

PITH: The white membrane under the skin of oranges, lemons, and other citrus fruits.

POTATOES: *Baking potatoes* are all-purpose potatoes that are picked as the main crop. *Boiling potatoes* are picked earlier in the season and have thinner skins.

SALSA: A prepared spicy Mexican sauce with different levels of hotness. Sometimes called picante sauce.

SPICES: The dried flowers, seeds, bark, or roots of plants used to add special flavors to foods. Available whole or ground to a powder.

VEGETABLE OIL SPRAY: Vegetable oil that's been packed in a spray can under pressure. It's sprayed on pots and pans to give them a light coating that will prevent foods from sticking.

NUTRIENT ANALYSES

How Our Recipes Are Analyzed

Each recipe in this book has been analyzed by computer for various nutrients. Each analysis includes all of the ingredients listed in the recipe, but does not include optional ingredients or foods suggested as accompaniments.

Each analysis is based on a single serving unless otherwise indicated. You'll find calculations for the number of calories, amount of protein, carbohydrates, cholesterol, sodium, calcium, total fat, saturated, polyunsaturated, and monounsaturated fatty acids per serving.

You may notice that the values for saturated, monounsaturated, and polyunsaturated fatty acids do not add up precisely to the total fat in the recipe. That's because the total fat includes not only the fatty acids but other fatty substances and glycerol. The values are as accurate as possible.

The caloric value is the number that remains after subtracting the energy cost (measured in calories) of digestion and metabolism.

Each recipe was analyzed with the type of oil listed with the ingredients. When a recipe calls for corn oil, you may, of course, use corn, safflower, or sunflower oil because they contain polyunsaturated fatty acids. When a recipe calls for margarine we used corn oil margarine for the analysis. When selecting margarine, remember to choose one that contains no more than 2 grams of saturated fat per tablespoon.

Serving sizes vary somewhat. When we say a soup serves 6 at 3/4 cup per serving, for example, that is approximate. When no serving size is given, assume that the dish is divided equally.

The nutrient and caloric breakdown of each recipe is based on the University of Minnesota Nutrition Coordinating Center's data base, which is derived primarily from information from the United States Department of Agriculture.

POP SNACK WITH APPLES
Nutrient Analysis

Calories		242 kcal
Protein		7 g
Carbohydrate		37 g
Total Fat		9 g
Saturated	1 g	
Polyunsaturated	3 g	
Monounsaturated	5 g	
Cholesterol		0 mg
Sodium		46 mg
Calcium		25 mg

NUTTY PINEAPPLE NIBBLES
Nutrient Analysis

Calories		92 kcal
Protein		3 g
Carbohydrate		8 g
Total Fat		6 g
Saturated	2 g	
Polyunsaturated	1 g	
Monounsaturated	2 g	
Cholesterol		9 mg
Sodium		109 mg
Calcium		26 mg

POP SNACK WITH PEACHES
Nutrient Analysis

Calories		264 kcal
Protein		8 g
Carbohydrate		42 g
Total Fat		10 g
Saturated	1 g	
Polyunsaturated	3 g	
Monounsaturated	5 g	
Cholesterol		0 mg
Sodium		40 mg
Calcium		29 mg

TORTILLA CRISPS
Nutrient Analysis

Calories		114 kcal
Protein		4 g
Carbohydrate		22 g
Total Fat		2 g
Saturated	0 g	
Polyunsaturated	1 g	
Monounsaturated	0 g	
Cholesterol		0 mg
Sodium		268 mg
Calcium		104 mg

TORTILLA CRISPS WITH MEXICAN SEASONING
Nutrient Analysis

Calories		120 kcal
Protein		4 g
Carbohydrate		23 g
Total Fat		2 g
Saturated	0 g	
Polyunsaturated	1 g	
Monounsaturated	0 g	
Cholesterol		0 mg
Sodium		168 mg
Calcium		114 mg

BAKED POTATO SOUP
Nutrient Analysis

Calories		202 kcal
Protein		9 g
Carbohydrate		35 g
Total Fat		3 g
Saturated	1 g	
Polyunsaturated	0 g	
Monounsaturated	1 g	
Cholesterol		4 mg
Sodium		557 mg
Calcium		128 mg

MEXI DIP OLÉ
Nutrient Analysis

Calories		111 kcal
Protein		9 g
Carbohydrate		11 g
Total Fat		4 g
Saturated	2 g	
Polyunsaturated	0 g	
Monounsaturated	1 g	
Cholesterol		12 mg
Sodium		248 mg
Calcium		284 mg

SUNSHINE SLAW
Nutrient Analysis

Calories		139 kcal
Protein		5 g
Carbohydrate		19 g
Total Fat		6 g
Saturated	1 g	
Polyunsaturated	2 g	
Monounsaturated	3 g	
Cholesterol		1 mg
Sodium		95 mg
Calcium		88 mg

GRANDPA'S FAVORITE SOUP
Nutrient Analysis

Calories		195 kcal
Protein		16 g
Carbohydrate		18 g
Total Fat		7 g
Saturated	2 g	
Polyunsaturated	2 g	
Monounsaturated	2 g	
Cholesterol		34 mg
Sodium		393 mg
Calcium		47 mg

SHIMMERING FRUIT SALAD
Nutrient Analysis

Calories		240 kcal
Protein		2 g
Carbohydrate		62 g
Total Fat		1 g
Saturated	0 g	
Polyunsaturated	0 g	
Monounsaturated	0 g	
Cholesterol		0 mg
Sodium		8 mg
Calcium		30 mg

GARDEN PATCH SOUP
Nutrient Analysis

Calories		136 kcal
Protein		7 g
Carbohydrate		15 g
Total Fat		5 g
Saturated	1 g	
Polyunsaturated	1 g	
Monounsaturated	2 g	
Cholesterol		0 mg
Sodium		715 mg
Calcium		34 mg

SHIMMERING FRUIT SALAD WITH PECANS
Nutrient Analysis

Calories		288 kcal
Protein		2 g
Carbohydrate		63 g
Total Fat		6 g
Saturated	1 g	
Polyunsaturated	1 g	
Monounsaturated	3 g	
Cholesterol		0 mg
Sodium		8 mg
Calcium		33 mg

SHAKE-IT-UP CHICKEN NUGGETS
Nutrient Analysis

Calories		348 kcal
Protein		30 g
Carbohydrate		19 g
Total Fat		16 g
Saturated	5 g	
Polyunsaturated	4 g	
Monounsaturated	6 g	
Cholesterol		68 mg
Sodium		668 mg
Calcium		134 mg

MICROWAVE LEMON FISH
Nutrient Analysis

Calories		245 kcal
Protein		26 g
Carbohydrate		4 g
Total Fat		14 g
Saturated	3 g	
Polyunsaturated	4 g	
Monounsaturated	5 g	
Cholesterol		45 mg
Sodium		299 mg
Calcium		47 mg

POLKA DOT CHICKEN PASTA SALAD
Nutrient Analysis

Calories		291 kcal
Protein		13 g
Carbohydrate		49 g
Total Fat		5 g
Saturated	1 g	
Polyunsaturated	2 g	
Monounsaturated	2 g	
Cholesterol		23 mg
Sodium		201 mg
Calcium		79 mg

TAMALE BEEF SQUARES
Nutrient Analysis

Calories		416 kcal
Protein		27 g
Carbohydrate		40 g
Total Fat		17 g
Saturated	6 g	
Polyunsaturated	3 g	
Monounsaturated	7 g	
Cholesterol		93 mg
Sodium		671 mg
Calcium		190 mg

MEXICAN SOMBREROS
Nutrient Analysis

Calories		186 kcal
Protein		20 g
Carbohydrate		15 g
Total Fat		5 g
Saturated	1 g	
Polyunsaturated	1 g	
Monounsaturated	1 g	
Cholesterol		47 mg
Sodium		343 mg
Calcium		114 mg

PASGETTI SPAGHETTI
Nutrient Analysis

Calories		156 kcal
Protein		5 g
Carbohydrate		27 g
Total Fat		3 g
Saturated	0 g	
Polyunsaturated	0 g	
Monounsaturated	2 g	
Cholesterol		0 mg
Sodium		204 mg
Calcium		37 mg

TASTY TURKEY CHILI
Nutrient Analysis

Calories		337 kcal
Protein		28 g
Carbohydrate		40 g
Total Fat		8 g
Saturated	2 g	
Polyunsaturated	3 g	
Monounsaturated	2 g	
Cholesterol		44 mg
Sodium		594 mg
Calcium		109 mg

BROILED ITALIAN MEATBALLS
Nutrient Analysis

Calories		267 kcal
Protein		26 g
Carbohydrate		10 g
Total Fat		13 g
Saturated	5 g	
Polyunsaturated	1 g	
Monounsaturated	6 g	
Cholesterol		112 mg
Sodium		430 mg
Calcium		156 mg

TOP HAT PIZZA
Nutrient Analysis

Calories		301 kcal
Protein		12 g
Carbohydrate		43 g
Total Fat		9 g
Saturated	3 g	
Polyunsaturated	3 g	
Monounsaturated	3 g	
Cholesterol		8 mg
Sodium		801 mg
Calcium		184 mg

CONFETTI-STUFFED TOMATO BOATS
Nutrient Analysis

Calories		127 kcal
Protein		8 g
Carbohydrate		13 g
Total Fat		6 g
Saturated	4 g	
Polyunsaturated	0 g	
Monounsaturated	2 g	
Cholesterol		18 mg
Sodium		237 mg
Calcium		133 mg

SPICY BUTTONS AND BOWS
Nutrient Analysis

Calories		294 kcal
Protein		12 g
Carbohydrate		37 g
Total Fat		11 g
Saturated	5 g	
Polyunsaturated	2 g	
Monounsaturated	3 g	
Cholesterol		18 mg
Sodium		512 mg
Calcium		224 mg

ORIENTAL STIR-FRY
Nutrient Analysis

Calories		83 kcal
Protein		1 g
Carbohydrate		14 g
Total Fat		3 g
Saturated	1 g	
Polyunsaturated	1 g	
Monounsaturated	1 g	
Cholesterol		0 mg
Sodium		52 mg
Calcium		28 mg

NUTTY BROCCOLI FLOWERS
Nutrient Analysis

Calories		113 kcal
Protein		4 g
Carbohydrate		7 g
Total Fat		9 g
Saturated	1 g	
Polyunsaturated	2 g	
Monounsaturated	5 g	
Cholesterol		0 mg
Sodium		152 mg
Calcium		66 mg

SPECKLED RICE
Nutrient Analysis

Calories		171 kcal
Protein		5 g
Carbohydrate		25 g
Total Fat		6 g
Saturated	1 g	
Polyunsaturated	1 g	
Monounsaturated	2 g	
Cholesterol		0 mg
Sodium		413 mg
Calcium		46 mg

FESTIVE PEAS
Nutrient Analysis

Calories		83 kcal
Protein		5 g
Carbohydrate		11 g
Total Fat		2 g
Saturated	1 g	
Polyunsaturated	1 g	
Monounsaturated	1 g	
Cholesterol		0 mg
Sodium		130 mg
Calcium		27 mg

CHEESY CORNBREAD
Nutrient Analysis

Calories		162 kcal
Protein		6 g
Carbohydrate		26 g
Total Fat		4 g
Saturated	1 g	
Polyunsaturated	1 g	
Monounsaturated	2 g	
Cholesterol		29 mg
Sodium		322 mg
Calcium		85 mg

CINNAMON-RAISIN SCONES
Nutrient Analysis

Calories		209 kcal
Protein		4 g
Carbohydrate		33 g
Total Fat		7 g
Saturated	2 g	
Polyunsaturated	2 g	
Monounsaturated	3 g	
Cholesterol		27 mg
Sodium		335 mg
Calcium		102 mg

TROPICAL FRUIT POPS
Nutrient Analysis

Calories		191 kcal
Protein		3 g
Carbohydrate		48 g
Total Fat		0 g
Saturated	0 g	
Polyunsaturated	0 g	
Monounsaturated	0 g	
Cholesterol		0 mg
Sodium		70 mg
Calcium		22 mg

SLUMBER PARTY FRENCH TOAST
Nutrient Analysis

Calories		268 kcal
Protein		6 g
Carbohydrate		41 g
Total Fat		9 g
Saturated	2 g	
Polyunsaturated	3 g	
Monounsaturated	4 g	
Cholesterol		1 mg
Sodium		342 mg
Calcium		77 mg

HIDDEN TREASURE CAKE
Nutrient Analysis

Calories		275 kcal
Protein		4 g
Carbohydrate		49 g
Total Fat		8 g
Saturated	2 g	
Polyunsaturated	2 g	
Monounsaturated	3 g	
Cholesterol		0 mg
Sodium		203 mg
Calcium		50 mg

ROSY CINNAMON APPLESAUCE
Nutrient Analysis

Calories		70 kcal
Protein		0 g
Carbohydrate		18 g
Total Fat		0 g
Saturated	0 g	
Polyunsaturated	0 g	
Monounsaturated	0 g	
Cholesterol		0 mg
Sodium		4 mg
Calcium		5 mg

GINGERSNAPS
Nutrient Analysis

Calories		102 kcal
Protein		1 g
Carbohydrate		16 g
Total Fat		4 g
Saturated	1 g	
Polyunsaturated	1 g	
Monounsaturated	2 g	
Cholesterol		7 mg
Sodium		55 mg
Calcium		13 mg

TROPICAL FRUIT SHERBET
Nutrient Analysis

Calories		259 kcal
Protein		3 g
Carbohydrate		66 g
Total Fat		0 g
Saturated	0 g	
Polyunsaturated	0 g	
Monounsaturated	0 g	
Cholesterol		0 mg
Sodium		72 mg
Calcium		30 mg

PUMPKIN CUSTARDS À LA MODE
Nutrient Analysis

Calories		252 kcal
Protein		12 g
Carbohydrate		40 g
Total Fat		5 g
Saturated	2 g	
Polyunsaturated	1 g	
Monounsaturated	1 g	
Cholesterol		11 mg
Sodium		376 mg
Calcium		305 mg

THREE SHAKES FOR BREAKFAST
SHAKE ONE—BANANA
Nutrient Analysis

Calories		287 kcal
Protein		20 g
Carbohydrate		49 g
Total Fat		2 g
Saturated	1 g	
Polyunsaturated	0 g	
Monounsaturated	1 g	
Cholesterol		11 mg
Sodium		433 mg
Calcium		361 mg

THREE SHAKES FOR BREAKFAST
SHAKE THREE—RASPBERRY
Nutrient Analysis

Calories		264 kcal
Protein		20 g
Carbohydrate		41 g
Total Fat		3 g
Saturated	1 g	
Polyunsaturated	1 g	
Monounsaturated	1 g	
Cholesterol		11 mg
Sodium		432 mg
Calcium		391 mg

THREE SHAKES FOR BREAKFAST
SHAKE TWO—STRAWBERRY-BANANA
Nutrient Analysis

Calories		268 kcal
Protein		20 g
Carbohydrate		43 g
Total Fat		3 g
Saturated	1 g	
Polyunsaturated	0 g	
Monounsaturated	1 g	
Cholesterol		11 mg
Sodium		434 mg
Calcium		373 mg

SUNSET PUNCH
Nutrient Analysis

Calories		161 kcal
Protein		1 g
Carbohydrate		40 g
Total Fat		0 g
Saturated	0 g	
Polyunsaturated	0 g	
Monounsaturated	0 g	
Cholesterol		0 mg
Sodium		11 mg
Calcium		25 mg

KIDS' QUESTIONNAIRE

Did you enjoy cooking the recipes in this *American Heart Association Kids' Cookbook*? Did you find one or two you found especially delicious and fun to make? We'd love to hear your comments! We'd also be pleased to receive one of your favorite original healthy recipes.

To share your thoughts and recipes with us, just fill out the form below or attach a separate sheet. Then mail it to us. We look forward to hearing from you.

Name: _____

Address: _____

Phone Number: _____

Which recipes did you try? _____

How easy or difficult were they to prepare? _____

What were your favorite recipes? _____

What did you like most about the book? _____

What did you like least about the book? _____

Do you have any other comments you'd like to make about the book? _____

_____

Do you have a recipe you'd like to share with us? _____
If so, please write it in the space below.

Name of Recipe:

Ingredients:

Equipment:

Instructions:

Thanks for your help. Please return this form to: American Heart Association
Consumer Publications Consultant
Office of Education and
Community Programs
Kids' Cookbook Questionnaire
7272 Greenville Avenue
Dallas, TX 75231-4596

INDEX